The evolution of Green Templeton College epitomises, and has contributed to, the evolution of both clinical medicine and the delivery of healthcare in the last 50 years. The work of Richard Doll firstly on cigarette smoking and then on the development of large scale randomised controlled trials was of central importance in changing medicine from being based on the opinion of the most senior doctor in the room to being based on best current evidence. The evolution of the randomised controlled trial also played a key part in the development of the amazing technologies of the last 50 years and this in turn created a huge challenge for health services to provide clinical services within the limits of the resources available. This led to the recognition of the need to develop the leadership and management of health services which have grown into a huge organisation tackling what is probably the most complex business on earth – healthcare.

This led to an appreciation of the need to manage resources effectively and the union of Green College and Templeton College has brought about a college which can play a leading role in the delivery and survival of universal healthcare globally. Uwe Kitzinger, one of the key figures in the development of Templeton College, with all its disciplines, was always very clear about the need to bring the disciplines together and the union of the two colleges provides Oxford, the United Kingdom and the world with a great resource for the challenges to come as need and demand continue to grow faster than the capacity of health services.

This history describes the evolution of the College with clarity and insight.

Sir Muir Gray CBE, Emeritus Fellow of Green Templeton College,
Director of the Optimal Ageing Programme at Oxford

This account captures very effectively the essence of what has been the evolution of Green Templeton College. As with many organisations, it is a picture of higgledy piggledy growth or perhaps a random walk culminating in the first merger of two Oxford Colleges in modern times.

Professor Michael Earl, Emeritus Fellow Green Templeton College
and former Dean of Templeton College

Professor Cranston, biographer of John Radcliffe, has told the tale of two colleges in a highly engaging style. From the building of the Radcliffe Observatory and its important contribution to astronomy to its conversion, first of all into a medical research centre with gruesome stories of alligators and sword-swallowers, and then into Green College for mainly medical students. Finally, he tells us about the genesis of Templeton College, which was dedicated to Management Studies and records how Templeton and Green merged to become Green Templeton College. The ins and outs of this complex history and the characters involved are described in a memorable way – a must read for all of us who have come to love Green Templeton College.

John Lennox, Emeritus Professor of Mathematics, University of Oxford,
Emeritus Fellow in Mathematics and Philosophy of Science, Green Templeton College

David's book provides an excellent insight into Green Templeton's wonderful Observatory, grounds and gardens. But more importantly, he has described, with careful research, the intriguing journey of how, over the last century, the two founding institutions, Green and Templeton Colleges, came about. The book provides an important narrative in the story of bringing to pre-eminence at Oxford University the life-changing disciplines of medicine and management. David shines a bright light on the pioneering and persevering spirit of the key people and institutions involved along the way.

Dr Keith Ruddle, Emeritus Fellow Green Templeton College
and former Templeton Fellow

Green-Templeton College emerged, a true silver lining, at the time of the move, from the comfort of the old Radcliffe Infirmary, hosting the medical students beloved Osler House up the hill to the John Radcliffe in Headington. The college has flourished, as documented brilliantly by David Cranston, in this new volume in his series, that continues to document the Oxford Medicine story.

Prof Alastair Buchan, Stroke Research, Radcliffe Department of Medicine,
University of Oxford

This important and lucid history is about a college that has enormous potential to produce the wise practitioners in health management of the future.

The Radcliffe Observatory is one of the most beautiful in the world and has told us much that is new, especially about the sun, and has partnered a project that has measured and understands the weather which now finds itself contributing to understanding climate change, something that is today more in need of such understanding than any other topic at any other time.

The Observatory was given to the Radcliffe Infirmary by Lord Nuffield, who also funded the School of Clinical Medicine with its Nuffield Professors. As was his hope, the research done thereafter prevented millions from dying from infection, head injury, post-partum haemorrhage, high blood pressure, type2 diabetes, and for 40 years in the Observatory it created an understanding of childbirth ,with measurement tools still in use to make the process safe for both mother and child.

The new campus, headed by the Observatory, is welcoming and its supporting literature talks about "what it is to be human" and about a relationship between Science and the Humanities.

The years of the completion of the building of the Observatory coincided with what now comes under the heading of One Health, the need to understand humans, animals, birds and insects as well as their environment.

By reading this history one learns about a site where Oxford University has made some astonishing and enormous contributions to health, wellbeing and happiness, and can be expected to continue to do so.

Professor Terence Ryan, Emeritus Fellow of Green Templeton College and Emeritus Professor of Dermatology, University of Oxford

David Cranston's several books have already vividly brought alive the histories of people and places in Oxford's medical story, from John Radcliffe himself to the pioneers of penicillin and transplantation. Here he describes the dynamic vision and leadership of those in two twentieth century Oxford colleges who aligned medical and social sciences with business and management studies to form and shape the vibrant and expanding Green Templeton College in 2008, whilst continuing to conserve its architecturally exquisite Radcliffe Observatory at the heart of the University's twenty-first century regeneration of the old Radcliffe Infirmary site.

Ian Baxter, Chair, Friends of the Radcliffe Observatory Quarter

I was delighted when I learnt that a book was being written that considered two quite different colleges , their history, contribution and how their merger took place. The book is full of wonderful details on each college, and it is full of surprises! In the world of academia, mergers between institutions mark complex transitions, uniting rich legacies and distinct traditions in the pursuit of new forms of impact. Executive education was the raison d'être of Templeton College, and the interdependence of theory and practice, the close relationships between academics and practitioners was the real living legacy of Templeton, one that it handed on to Green. Green College was a hub for interdisciplinary scholarship and a strong shaping presence in medical education and practice, which proved a rich environment for exploring leadership challenges for Templeton Fellows and students. This book captures the essence of the merger and charts the journey of these remarkable colleges. The book is a testament to the remarkable capacity of Oxford to adapt and respond to global challenges. It is a story of blending past challenges and traditions, building on lessons learnt in forging a shared future.

Sue Dopson, Deputy Dean for People and EDI, Rhodes Trust Professor of Organisational Behaviour, Fellow of Green Templeton College

Green Templeton
The Legacy of
Two Colleges

David Cranston completed his medical training in Bristol and worked in Exeter and Bath before coming to Oxford for postgraduate doctoral research.

He is a Fellow of the Royal College of Surgeons of England and spent 30 years as Consultant Urological and Transplant Surgeon in Oxford. He is Emeritus Associate Professor of Surgery in the Nuffield Department of Surgical Science and Emeritus Fellow of Green Templeton College, Oxford.

Outside medicine he serves as a licensed lay minister in the Church of England and is Co-Chaplain at the Oxford Centre for Mission Studies.

FOREWORD

Since I began my tenure as Principal of Green Templeton College in 2020 I have greatly benefitted from the wisdom and experience of David Cranston and his peers as Emeritus Fellows for a grounding in the rich history of the college and its antecedents.

While it may seem perverse in a university with eight centuries of history to be telling the story of a fourteen-year-old modern invention in the collegiate system, David shows readers why this is a heritage worth recognising.

He draws on invaluable oral testimony with members from across Green College, Templeton College and the Oxford Centre for Management Studies. This is particularly welcome while the founding fellows remain to tell the story of the development of Green Templeton for future generations.

The heritage of the colleges is particularly interesting in light of what has developed in Oxford over the past half century.

This is true with the explosion of the university as a global epicentre for the future of medicine and medical science. From the COVID and malaria vaccines to the future of medical teaching, the college and its members have been major contributors to a number of pioneering developments.

It is equally true for the development and standing of business and management education. The evolution of the Saïd Business School into a globally recognised hub of learning, builds on a history spearheaded by the Oxford

Centre for Management Studies and subsequently Templeton College.

I have no doubt that this will be the first of a number of histories of Green Templeton College and David's contribution provides an invaluable perspective for others to draw on and supplement in the decades ahead.

At the same time, as I write in early 2025, Green Templeton is looking to new horizons. We have ambitious plans for the future of the college and are on the cusp of launching a major fundraising campaign to deliver them.

It will be an exciting period ahead, building on the hard work of the past few years to put our vision of the college's future together and to build on the legacy of those that went before.

Sir Michael Dixon
Principal, Green Templeton College

ACKNOWLEDGEMENTS

I am grateful to Professor Sir Michael Dixon for his foreword and to Sir Muir Gray for his suggestion that this book should be written in the first place. Many people have helped with this book, in particular Fellows of both Templeton College and Green College who have shared their respective memories with me. In particular Dorothy Cooke, Michael Earl, Stephen Barclay, Keith Ruddle, Sue Dopson, Gerald Chambers, Alastair Buchan, Julian Britton, Clive Hahn, Gordon Stirrat, Mike Gilmer, Chris Adams, and John Lennox. Michael Pirie has an intricate knowledge of the Observatory and the related buildings, as well as looking after the gardens, and Appendix 3 in particular is based on his research and knowledge.

Lindy Castell has patiently proof-read several drafts and Valerie Petts has allowed me to reproduce some of her beautiful watercolours that have been used in my other books. Tony Gray has been very helpful and patient as both editor and publisher through his company WORDS BY DESIGN. Lastly, but by no means least, I am grateful to my wife Rosie for her support over 47 years of marriage.

Dedication

To all the staff of Green Templeton College both seen and unseen who allow the College to function so well.

Contents

PREFACE

I was a relative late arrival at Green College coming in 2007 just before the merger with Templeton College. However, I was very familiar with the Radcliffe Infirmary, having operated in the Towler Theatres on many occasions, often in the middle of the night in my role as a transplant surgeon. Over the years I have been intrigued by the legacy of John Radcliffe as well as the philanthropic donations of Lord Nuffield and I was also privileged to know some of those who developed penicillin in the 1940s, in particular Norman Heatley and Lady Margaret Florey. The Radcliffe Quarter with the new Stephen A Schwarzman Centre for the Humanities and the potential move of the University administrative centre to the old Radcliffe Infirmary site means that Green Templeton College will truly be at the heart of the University, and if the South Entrance to the Observatory is reopened in the next few years, it will be a return it to its original status.

While I knew a lot about Green College, I knew very little about Templeton College, and it has been a journey of discovery to document its history with the help of many of the Templeton Fellows. It was interesting to note that the Oxford Centre for Management Studies began on the Woodstock Road back in 1965.

Green Templeton College is the caretaker for one of the most iconic buildings in Oxford and as Professor Irene Tracy, Vice-Chancellor of Oxford University has said:

With its long and illustrious history, the Observatory is truly an Oxford landmark. Its conservation is essential so that future generations can benefit from all it has to offer.

My hope is that this book will play a role in both capturing and preserving both the history of the Radcliffe Quarter and the background to the foundation of Green Templeton College.

David Cranston
January 2025

INTRODUCTION

Green Templeton College was established in its current form in October 2008 through the merger of Green College and Templeton College. Green College was founded in 1977 with its doors opening in 1979, on the current college site in Woodstock Road, as a postgraduate college, leading the way in medical and applied social sciences. The Oxford Centre for Management Studies had already established business and management education in Oxford from 1965, initially based in a house which was also on the Woodstock Road, and moving to the purpose-built Kennington site on the southern edge of the city in 1969. Templeton College was inaugurated on that site in 1984 following support from Sir John Templeton (1912–2008), and it continued the rapid development of business and management education at Oxford, bringing together global leaders from many diverse fields. The resultant merger of Green and Templeton Colleges has led to it being a place of engagement of both academics and professionals from different areas in relation to health sciences, management and ecology.

The unique eighteenth century Radcliffe Observatory is the central focus of the College which covers three acres of ground to the north of Oxford city centre along the Woodstock Road, in what is now known as the Radcliffe Observatory Quarter. Begun in 1772, the Observatory was paid for by the Radcliffe Trustees from money left by the philanthropy of Dr John Radcliffe (1652-1714). His legacy also paid for the construction

The Radcliffe Observatory

of the Radcliffe Infirmary next door. To understand the origins of Green Templeton College properly we need to begin with John Radcliffe and take a journey through the history of Oxford Medicine and the building of the Observatory.

JOHN RADCLIFFE

The name of Dr John Radcliffe,[1] the most famous physician of his day, continues to echo across the city of Oxford in the names of the John Radcliffe Hospital, the Radcliffe Camera, the Radcliffe Observatory and, for over two centuries, until its closure in 2007, the Radcliffe Infirmary. So who was this man who left such a generous legacy to Oxford?

John Radcliffe was probably born in 1652. His parents had a son, John, born

John Radcliffe

in 1650 who died and, as often happened in those days, the next son was given the same name. John Radcliffe made his name as a physician in Oxford where his greatest success came with the treatment of Lady Spencer, an ancestor of Princess Diana. Lady Spencer's husband, Sir Thomas, was Lord of the nearby Manor of Yarnton. He had been ill for a number of years, although it is not recorded what ailed him. Lady Spencer's son-

---

1 For further reading see Cranston, D, *John Radcliffe and his Legacy to Oxford*. Words by Design, 2013.

in-law came to hear of Radcliffe's success and persuaded her to call him in to treat her husband. Radcliffe came and prescribed, and within three weeks Sir Thomas was fitter than he had been for many years. As a result of this success, Radcliffe found his services in demand from many noble families in the area. Sir Thomas subsequently died in 1685 at the age of 47 and the marble tomb erected in his memory by his wife can be seen today in Yarnton parish church.

In 1684 Radcliffe decided to move to London and there seek his fortune as a physician. His rise to fame was rapid, partly due to his force of character and diagnostic acumen. However, his move to London may also have been connected with a state visit paid to Oxford in the spring of 1683 by James Duke of York, later James II, in the company of his second wife and unmarried daughter, the Princess Anne. Radcliffe probably met her through Obadiah Walker, Master of University College, Radcliffe's *alma mater*.

Two years after arriving in London, Princess Anne's father, King James II, selected Radcliffe as his daughter's physician. She had already lost three children when Radcliffe took over her care. The fourth child, William Duke of Gloucester, was the only one of her 17 children to survive infancy. When he was four he had a serious illness and Radcliffe saved his life and was presented with 1,000 guineas from the Princess. In 1700, two years before her accession, Radcliffe was summoned to Windsor at a late stage to treat the Duke, then aged eleven, but was unable to save him and he died. Although the cause of death is uncertain, it was probably due to smallpox.

Radcliffe was also consulted at a late stage for the last illness of Queen Mary in 1694, but was unable to save her. He is reported as saying bluntly that her treatment had been wrong. Some blamed him for her death, but he was later exonerated when it was found that he was called in only when she was close to death from smallpox. Nevertheless, King William still consulted and employed Radcliffe for a while, until the occasion when Radcliffe examined the King's swollen legs and exclaimed, *"Why, truly, I would not have your Majesty's two legs for your three kingdoms."* This exhausted the King's patience with him and he was never officially consulted again.

Twice Radcliffe contemplated marriage and when nearly 60 he fell in love with one of his patients, but with his benefactions to Oxford in mind he said that, *"truly he had an old one to think of"* and he did not want to share his fortune with another.

In London he was earning 20 guineas a day for his work and indeed he would sometimes charge this amount to visit a patient. If a patient sent a servant to him for advice, his charge was two guineas for the first visit, one for the second, two for the third, and so forth.

Radcliffe died in 1714 and The Historical Register of 1714 reports his death as follows:

> *Died John Radcliffe, MD, Member of Parliament for Buckingham, accounted the most eminent Physician this England ever produced. He was a man of good sense, sound judgement, and admirable skill in his art, chiefly founded on the Best Mistress, Experience.*

His body was taken from London to Oxford and lay in state in the Divinity School in Oxford before being carried, by the Bishops of Bristol and Chester, the Master of University College, the Regius Professor of Divinity and the Professor of Law, past Brasenose, Lincoln, Exeter and Jesus Colleges to the Northgate, and back via Carfax to St Mary's Church. Following the service in the University Church of St Mary's, the body was buried in a vault in front of the organ loft on the north of the entrance to the chancel. For over 100 years there was no inscription to commemorate him or mark his tomb, but in 1819 a grave was dug next to Radcliffe's and the plate on Radcliffe's coffin was seen for the first time since his burial. Today a plaque can be seen in the University Church marking the place of his coffin.

He died worth £140,000 (£23m today). He had given £40,000 to the University for building an additional library to the Bodleian (The Radcliffe Camera) and to furnish it with books and pay for a librarian. He had left £5,000 to University College for travelling fellowships[2] which he had entered as a member in 1665, and after his death the Radcliffe Trust was set up which remains in place today.

Sir William Osler, Regius Professor of Medicine in Oxford at the beginning of the twentieth century, said of Radcliffe:

> *One lesson learned from his life is that if you do not write, then make money; and, after you finish, leave it ...to charity.*

Nine years after Radcliffe's death, his contemporary, Sir Christopher Wren, was laid to rest in St Paul's Cathedral. The words written on the stone plaque over Wren's tomb in the crypt of the greatest building he designed could equally well have been written of John Radcliffe with respect to buildings that he was responsible for in Oxford.

> *Lector, si monumentum requires, circumspice.*
> *Reader, if you seek his memorial, look around you.*

Today the bronze statue of John Radcliffe by sculptor Martin Jennings stands on the South lawn of the Radcliffe Observatory, facing the new Stephen A Schwarzman Centre for the Humanities.

---

2 The Radcliffe Travelling Fellowship continue to this day, one of the more recent being Sir Roger Bannister, the first man to run a mile in under four minutes at the Iffley Road running track in Oxford in 1954. He was an acclaimed neurologist practicing in London and later Master of Pembroke College Oxford.

THE RADCLIFFE OBSERVATORY

In 1619, Henry Savile, a mathematician, classical scholar and Warden of Merton College, established the position of Savilian Professor of Astronomy at Oxford. He founded two positions in mathematics and astronomy, subjects described as *"almost totally unknown and abandoned in England."* One of the early holders of that title from 1661–1673 was Sir Christopher Wren who, apart from designing St Paul's Cathedral in London and the Sheldonian Theatre in Oxford, also designed the Royal Observatory at Greenwich, which was established in 1675.

Christopher Wren did not think a separate building was needed for an Observatory in Oxford, saying that *"an adequate observatory could be placed as well in a garden as in a tower."* Indeed, such a structure was built in 1705 by Professor Edmond Halley, also a Savilian professor, on the roof of his residence in New College Lane where it can still be seen today. Another Observatory was built at Corpus Christi College by Thomas Hornsby, also a Savilian Professor, but in 1768 Hornsby asked the Radcliffe Trustees for money to build a proper Observatory and

New College Lane Observatory

plans were laid down for a three-stage tower with an adjacent building for the larger instruments.³

Fifty two years earlier, in 1716, Halley suggested that a precise measurement of the distance between the Earth and the Sun could be calculated by timing the transit of Venus across the surface of the sun from widely separated observing stations on earth.

It is for that reason that James Cook and astronomer Charles Green set sail for Tahiti in 1768 to observe the transit

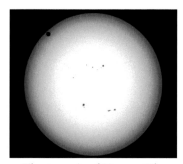

The transit of Venus. The black dot of Venus is seen top left as it begins its transit

of Venus from there, while Hornsby viewed it from Oxford on the 3ʳᵈ of June 1769. If the distance between the Sun and the Earth could be calculated, it would provide scientists with key information for establishing the size of the Universe and would be able to improve the accuracy of European navigation across the globe by accurately calculating longitude.⁴ It also solved some of the debate about the exact equivalence between English yard versus the French metre.⁵

When Hornsby became the Savilian Professor of Astronomy, he also gave correct details of the latitude of Oxford (51° 45 minutes 15 seconds) and also the longitude of Oxford (5 minutes 3 seconds to the West of Greenwich), based on a comparison of his observations of the sun's eclipse in

Oxford and observations made at Greenwich. This is the reason that 'Christ Church Time', is five minutes different from Greenwich Mean Time (GMT). Great Tom chimes 101 times at 9.05pm, which corresponds with 9.00pm GMT. In 1852 Greenwich Mean Time was formally adopted nationwide, but Christ Church steadfastly retained 'Oxford' time, five minutes behind GMT.

The first steps towards the construction of the Radcliffe Observatory began in 1771 on the current site, after the Radcliffe Trustees agreed to fund the building. A site was needed which was reasonably far from the centre of Oxford at the time, to minimise atmospheric pollution. The present site was chosen in 1770 when the Radcliffe Infirmary had just opened, allowing the Radcliffe Trustees to turn their attention from the hospital to the building of the Observatory. The fourth Duke of Marlborough had a passionate interest in astronomy and offered a gift of land adjacent to the Radcliffe Infirmary as a site for the Observatory.

Construction of the Observatory

It took another 22 years to complete the whole project, by which time the cost had risen to over £31,000, nearly three times the sum proposed in 1771 – a remarkably familiar story three centuries later!

The foundation stone for the Observatory was laid in June 1772. The architect Henry Keene was initially taken on to design the Observatory, and the Observer's House at least was his work, but he was superseded by James Wyatt in 1773, who introduced the idea of the Tower of the Winds,

The Athens Tower of the Winds

which had been built in Athens c50-40 BC, to crown the building. Wyatt used the engravings of James Stuart and Nicholas Revett that had only recently appeared in their monumental work *The Antiquities of Athens* (1762) as the basis for his design of the Tower, partly because it was orientated on the points of the compass, just as the Observatory had to be.

Wyatt placed his Tower of the Winds above a semi-circular central building with its arc facing north. This central semi-circle provides space for an entrance hall at the foot of the stairwell and for two other side rooms, originally for the Observer and his assistant. Until 1818 it was the best Observatory in Europe and it remained in the top four until 1830. It certainly was, and remains, a beautiful building and provided a very comfortable house for the Observer and an 'all weather' passage to the Observatory (from the Observer's House).

Thomas Hornsby, the first Savilian Professor to work at the Observatory, made many thousands of astronomical readings during his time there, but they were not published until the

The exterior of the Observatory is decorated with allegorical figures.
Painting by Valerie Petts.

1920s. Later pollution became more of a problem, and the first act of parliament was passed to manage the excess smoke pollution due to the Industrial Revolution, although it is possible that smoke fires from the colleges and other buildings may have been more of an issue in Oxford.

The exterior of the Observatory is decorated with allegorical figures (see previous page). On the roof is a globe supported by two figures, Atlas and Hercules. In Greek mythology Atlas was a Titan, condemned to support the heavens on his head and hands for eternity on Mount Atlas as a punishment for taking part in a revolt against Zeus and the Olympians. Hercules, as one of his twelve labours, was asked to bring three golden apples from the garden of Hesperides, protected by a 100-headed dragon and, in order to get the apples, he persuaded Atlas to pick them up while he temporarily took over the burden of supporting the world. Atlas is supposed to have taught Hercules about astronomy, hence their position above the Observatory

Atlas and Hercules supporting the globe on the roof of the Observatory

THE EIGHT WINDS AT RADCLIFFE OBSERVATORY

The figures of the eight winds seen on the top of the Tower of the Observatory appeared on the original Tower of the Winds in Athens, although Oxford is the only place in the world where the names of the eight winds are inserted below each of the carvings in brass lettering.

The figures of the eight einds

The engravings of James Stuart and Nicholas Revett were used by the sculptor John Bacon (1740-99) as the basis for his designs for the flying figures round the top of the stonework of the Observatory. On the top of the original Tower of the Winds in Athens was Triton, Greek god of the sea, statue of half-man, half-fish. He is not present on the Observatory but he can still be seen adjacent to the College in the forecourt fountain of the former Radcliffe Infirmary.

Triton on the fountain of the former Radcliffe Infirmary

The eight personified winds round the top of the building, regarded as deities are:

Boreas, *the cold North wind from which the name for Aurora Borealis is derived.*

Notos, *the South wind, the Sirocco of modern Italy.*

Zephyros, *the gentle West wind.*

Euros, *the South East wind, warm and rain bringing.*

Kaikias, *the North East wind, which tips hailstones.*

Skiron, *the North West wind dries up vegetation.*

Apeliotes, *the East wind, bringing mild weather and gentle rain.*

Lips, *the South West wind, prevented ships from sailing out as it blew straight into Piraeus harbour.*

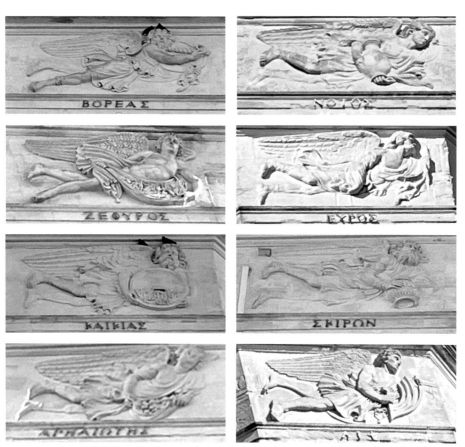

The eight winds

The twelve signs of the zodiac are also seen at the top of the second story of the Observatory. These do not appear on the original Tower of the Winds in Athens. Neither do the three panels representing morning, noon and evening which are set between the last four zodiac signs on the North face of the Observatory. The morning panel on the East face has three figures: Eos (Dawn) carries a pitcher in her right hand as a container for morning dew and a lamp lit by the Morning Star (Venus); the central panel on the North face is a single figure of Helios (the Sun) standing in his four-horse chariot at the noon tide zenith of his journey across the sky; the panel on the West

15

Morning, noon and evening

face represents the approach of night and the two-horse chariot is identifiable as Nyx (night) by the veil over her head and the stars which surround her.

The entrance hall of the Observatory was originally entered from the south through a porch modelled directly on the entrance to the Tower of the Winds in Athens. In due course it became the College common room and subsequently the College dining room, and as the new Radcliffe Observatory Quarter

The entrance hall

takes shape, the plan is that it will retake its place as the entrance to the Observatory.

Next to the main dining room is a smaller private dining room called the Grzeslo Room, in honour of Ignacy Grzeslo, a Polish inventor who amongst other things designed a machine to measure the flow through a gas pipeline more accurately. His gift allowed a major restoration of the Radcliffe Observatory.

The elliptical staircase representing the orbit of the planets has no central support and is an architectural feat of engineering. It rises past the College common room to a few feet below the top floor which is the most beautiful part of the building, inspired by the model of a Roman domed rotunda. Flooded with light from tall windows, it still has the Georgian glass in place, with a beautifully patterned ceiling and is often

Looking down the staircase (left) and looking up into the rotunda

The Radcliffe Observatory, by Valerie Petts

Former Principal David Watson looking out of the window in the Tower

too cold in winter and too hot in the summer. Two of the windows on the east and west sides of the Tower could be opened from floor level to allow telescopes to be taken out onto the adjoining roofs. A further iron stairway rises to the highest viewing point where the 1814 Ackerman print of Oxford as viewed from there can be seen. Over 200 years later, the Oxford skyline remains largely unchanged.

Astronomical Observatory 1814

This stairway is an example of the artistic aspect of iron engineering during the Industrial Revolution. The pattern of the ironwork can be seen in many of the cities of the British Empire of that era, particularly on the balconies of homes such as in Paddington, a suburb of Sydney. This is because the sailing ships of that time needed ballast and it was easy to manoeuvre iron into the depths of the ships and therefore easy to transport it all over the world.

The Tower has featured in a number of films. The BBC television series of *Morse* and *Lewis*, for example, included 'The Lions of Nemea' which saw the ceiling of the small Rotunda next door to be covered with stars!

The Tower still has some of the original Georgian furnishings, including a mahogany ladder and a set of steps and mahogany chairs.

The Duke of Marlborough Telescope, also known as the Marlborough-Tulley Telescope, which can be seen in the room, was given to John Spencer-Churchill, the 7th Duke of Marlborough, in 1844. He was Winston Churchill's grandfather and a trustee of the Radcliffe

Duke of Marlborough Telescope

Observatory who was initially given the telescope for use at Blenheim Palace. It became known as the Duke of Marlborough Telescope after the Duke's death, when his widow, the Dowager Duchess of Marlborough, gave it to the Radcliffe Observer, Edward Stone, in 1884, who was desperate for new instruments. Stone used it for observations from the Radcliffe Observatory in the late nineteenth century, and it was ideal for this purpose because it was a small instrument that could be manoeuvred out onto the balconies.

The telescope was the first to successfully image the chromosphere or Sun's inner atmosphere in fine detail. The two lenses at the objective or 'sky' end helped to correct for aberrations, resulting in superb clarity and the ability to separate the images of close objects, for example, double stars.

In 1896 Edward Stone took the Marlborough Telescope with him to view the total solar eclipse from the Novaya Zemlya archipelago in the Arctic Ocean because of its excellent optics and portable nature.

It remained at the Radcliffe Observatory until 1935, when, under the direction of Harold Knox-Shaw, the last UK-based Radcliffe Observer, it was relocated to Pretoria, South Africa.

In 2009 it was rediscovered, unused, in a box in the office of Professor Philip Charles, then Director of the South African Astronomical Observatory. After a series of negotiations, on 1st June 2012, just before the College's celebrations to mark the last twenty-first century transit of Venus, the telescope was returned to the Radcliffe Observatory where it now stands on long term loan in its original position. A further donation was made in 2024 when Emeritus Fellow in Mathematics, Professor John Lennox, presented the College with a 10-inch computer controlled reflector telescope. The other older instruments of the Observatory are now displayed in the Museum of the History of Science in Broad Street Oxford.

Thomas Hornsby and his family moved into the Observer's House in 1773. The lecture room on the first floor of the

Thomas Hornsby

Stephen Rigaud

Manuel Johnson

Robert Main

Radcliffe Observers

1773-1810 Thomas Hornsby
1810-1826 Abraham Robertson (no image)
1827-1839 Stephen Rigaud
1839-1859 Manuel Johnson
1860-1878 Robert Main

Edward Stone

Arthur Rambaut

Harold Knox-Shaw

David Thackeray

Radcliffe Observers

1879-1897 Edward Stone
1897-1924 Arthur Rambaut
1924-1950 Harold Knox-Shaw
1950-1974 David Thackeray

Observatory was completed in 1789, while the observing room above it, which was to accommodate the portable instruments used for observing beyond the meridian, was completed in 1794.

Hornsby died in 1810 at the age of 76 in the Observer's House and was succeeded by Abraham Robertson who, in turn, was succeeded in 1827 by 53-year-old Stephen Rigaud. However, his happiness in gaining the Savilian Chair and Observer's House was shattered the next year when his young wife died in March 1828 leaving him with seven young children to support. It was remarked that his hair turned white overnight. He died suddenly on the 16th of March 1839 and was succeeded by Manuel Johnson, who earlier in his career, on the 27th of July 1832, had observed the total solar eclipse while in charge of the Ladder Hill Observatory on St Helena.

There was a separation of the Savilian Professorship from the Radcliffe Observatory at this time when the University chose its own Savilian Professor and the Radcliffe Trustees went their own way in choosing Manuel Johnson as their new astronomer. Thus from 1839 the Radcliffe Observatory became independent, although the Observer might do some University teaching in the west wing. In 1842 Manuel Johnson completed the publication of his book of *Astronomical Observations Made at the Radcliffe Observatory Oxford in the Year 1840*. His preface opens with the following words:

> *The building of the Radcliffe Observatory was begun about the year 1771, and in 1774 was sufficiently advanced to receive the instruments which had been prepared for it, though the works were not entirely completed before the year 1794.*
>
> *It owes its origin in a great measure to the exertions of the late Dr Hornsby, who, being at the time Savilian Professor of Astronomy, called the attention of the University Authorities to the subject. Through them an application was made to the Radcliffe Trustees, who*

ASTRONOMICAL OBSERVATIONS

MADE AT THE

RADCLIFFE OBSERVATORY,

OXFORD,

IN THE YEAR 1840.

BY

MANUEL J. JOHNSON, M.A.

RADCLIFFE OBSERVER.

VOL. I.

PUBLISHED BY ORDER OF THE RADCLIFFE TRUSTEES.

OXFORD,
PRINTED BY W. BAXTER.
JOHN HENRY PARKER.
1842.

generously consented to bear the entire expense of the building and furnishing one of the largest, and, at that time, probably the best equipped Observatory in Europe.

Robert Main succeeded Johnson in 1860 and in 1870 published the observations of 1854-61 as the second Radcliffe catalogue of 2,386 stars.

After 1861 the astronomical work of the Radcliffe Observatory became less important as it had no first-class instruments and, in 1874, a new Observatory was established in the University Parks less than a mile away. Edward Stone took over as observer in 1879 and Arthur Rambaut in 1898. They in turn were followed by Harold Knox-Shaw (1924 to

The Observatory in University Parks

1950), who, because of pollution, found that less than 30 nights a year in Oxford were conducive for photography, and in 1928 was seeking support to move the observatory to a site in South Africa. This was agreed with the Radcliffe Trustees who put the Observatory up for sale in 1929 for the non-negotiable sum of £100,000.

This potential move coincided with the fact that the Governing Body of the Radcliffe Infirmary adjacent to the Observatory, chaired by Mr William Morris (later Lord Nuffield), was desperate to expand, and the only possibility was to move onto the nine-acre Observatory site. When William Morris heard that the Observatory was likely to move to South Africa, he bought the Observatory site from the Radcliffe Trustees for the agreed sum of £100,000, although it was also agreed

William Morris

that the Observatory would continue with astronomical work until 1934, when it would become the Nuffield Institute of Medical Research.

In recent years, Professor Terence Ryan met Jane Dowling, an artist and teacher at the Ruskin School, who as a young girl of ten walked in the company of Lord Nuffield and a group of physicians from Guy's Hospital, including her father, on Nuffield's Golf Course at Huntercombe. She remembered Nuffield talking about his own health and contrasting the research carried out at Guy's Hospital with the lack of research carried out at the Radcliffe Infirmary in Oxford due to a lack of space.

Like John Radcliffe three centuries earlier, Lord Nuffield transformed the medical environment of Oxford, becoming one of the most influential philanthropists of the twentieth century.[6] He began his life repairing and then making bicycles. Subsequently he made motorbikes and then made cars, producing his first Bullnose Morris in 1912. The MG (Morris Garage) remains the insignia of many cars still produced today.

---

6 See Cranston D, Morris PJ, *Lord Nuffield and his Double Legacy*. Words by Design, 2018.

THE WEATHER STATION

James Bradley

Meteorology started in Oxford with James Bradley who was the Savilian Professor of Astronomy from 1721 until his death in 1762. He discovered that light waves bend as they pass from the vacuum of space into the earth's atmosphere, and as a result of this, the apparent direction of a star can be displaced – similar to that of an image viewed underwater – and the amount of displacement depends not only on the observed altitude of the star, but also the pressure and temperature of the atmosphere at the point of observation. Therefore in order to obtain a correct observation of the stars, it is necessary to understand the atmospheric effect and adjust the readings accordingly.

Thomas Hornsby is known to have made regular meteorological observations in 1767 from the roof of the house in New College Lane where Edmond Halley had built a small teaching laboratory, but his meteorological observations from the new Radcliffe Observatory started in 1774, shortly after his appointment as the first Radcliffe Observer, when the ground floor rooms had been built. Here he used a 12-inch copper funnel as his rain gauge and a barometer made in 1773. An unbroken daily air temperature record exists from November 1813, daily rainfall from January 1827 and sunshine

The weather station in 1929 (courtesy the Topical Press Agency),
and (below) the weather station today

from February 1880. These are the longest single-site weather records in the United Kingdom, and amongst the longest in the world. They are particularly valuable because the instruments in use and their exposure have been fully documented throughout. There were some issues to be resolved – such as should rain be collected on the roof or on the ground – and if the latter, should measurements be in the shadow of the Observatory or further away.

Publication of the meteorological observations in the annual volumes of the *Radcliffe Astronomical Observations* commenced in 1849, daily readings being published from 1853 until cessation of the *Radcliffe Observations* series in 1935.

In the 1850s, the meteorological instruments began to be updated, and the siting and frequency of observation improved. Instruments were brought into use to provide continuous records of temperature, wind and rainfall.

In 1872 the Radcliffe Observatory became a reporting station to the meteorological office in London. From 1873 to 1913 its daily meteorological observations were telegraphed to the meteorological office to contribute to the preparation of synoptic charts and reports.

Since 1881 reliable records exist of all observations made until today, except for soil temperatures, which have only been recorded since 1925, and temperatures of the concrete surface which have been recorded since 1987. All observations are to the standards laid down by the Meteorological Office, by whom the site is regularly inspected.

By 1934, at the time of the Nuffield Institute for Medical Research, the anemometers were still kept on the roof. There was an exit through a wooden door in the Tower of the Winds and a rather rickety wooden staircase up to the roof of the Observatory where one could walk around in a drainage gully that had no railings.

The Observatory experienced some of the most extreme weather in the very cold winters of 1957 and 1963, when one of the users of the Observatory spent days in his naval great coat. It was not until the advent of Green College that the Observatory turned its face to the North and opened its doors to what was to become the College garden.

Until 1935, when the Radcliffe Astronomical Observatory moved to Pretoria, meteorological observations were a subsidiary task of the Radcliffe Observer and his staff. Since 1935 the meteorological work has been under the direction of the University of Oxford, delegated to the School of Geography. From 1st July 1935 the station's official title has been 'The Radcliffe Meteorological Station, Oxford'.

With the publication in 2019 by Stephen and Tim Burt of *Oxford Weather and Climate since 1767*, the full Radcliffe record was published for the first time.

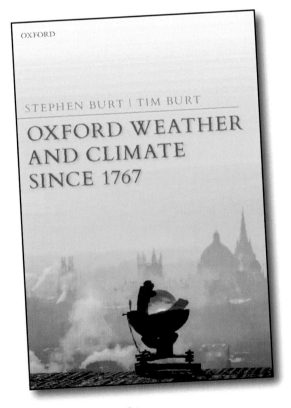

MEDICINE IN OXFORD

Adjacent to Green Templeton College was the Grade II listed building which for many years was Oxford's only hospital, The Radcliffe Infirmary. Over the years it has been intimately linked with The Radcliffe Observatory and, until its closure as a hospital in 2007, with Green College.

The first proposals to build a new hospital for Oxford were made in 1758 at a meeting of the Radcliffe Trustees. The sum of £4,000 was released for the new hospital, which was subsequently constructed on land given by the Member of Parliament for Oxford, Thomas Rowney. The Radcliffe

The Radcliffe Infirmary in 1835

The Radcliffe Infirmary by Valerie Petts

Infirmary was opened on St Luke's Day, 1770, at a final cost of £12,791, again, three times the estimated cost!

Patients suffering from smallpox or any infectious disease were not admitted. Neither were patients with epilepsy, ulcers, inoperable cancers, tuberculosis or dropsy. Pregnant women, children under seven (except for major operations) and the mentally ill were also barred.

The honorary physicians and surgeons gave their services free, maintaining themselves by private practice, although there were junior doctors on the paid staff. The hospital depended on voluntary giving, and larger donations conferred the status of Governor, with the right to elect officers and recommend patients. A patient could only be admitted on a Governor's 'turn', a system which was ended officially in 1884. Some of the Governors continued to claim their right to admit patients until 1920, when a 2d per week Contributory Scheme was introduced. Within three years this was providing 60 percent of the hospital's income.

There had been links between medicine and the University since 1546 when the first Regius Professor of Medicine, John Warner, was appointed by King Henry VIII. By 2000 there had been 30 holders of this office, and it remains a crown appointment today. In the early days these people were often nonentities who lived a quiet life but that changed when Sir William Osler (1849-1919) was appointed Regius Professor in 1904. He was a Canadian who was one of the founding fathers of Johns Hopkins Hospital in Baltimore, a man of charm and energy with a high reputation for teaching and clinical ability.[7]

During his time and up to the mid-1930s the Radcliffe Infirmary was a typical provincial hospital serving about a quarter of a million people, and there was no inclination to do research there. This worried William Osler, the first doctor

---

7 See Cranston, D, *William Osler and His Legacy to Medicine*. Words by Design, 2017.

with experience of hospital management to chair its committee of management.

Although there were undergraduate students in Oxford, they completed their course of clinical training in London, Liverpool or Birmingham, although William Osler organised ward rounds for them on a Sunday which were so popular that clinical students came up to Oxford from London for them. The students also had to return to

William Osler

Oxford to take their final examination for the Oxford degree of Bachelor of Medicine (BM) and Bachelor of Surgery (BCh), held twice a year, which included the examination of outpatients and inpatients at the Radcliffe Infirmary.

Osler's successor was Sir Archibald Garrod who held the post from 1920-28. He was an exceptional scientist whose book *The Inborn Errors of Metabolism*, published in 1909, was said to mark the beginning of medical genetics.

Osler and Garrod were keen to establish Oxford as a clinical medical school, but the University was indifferent and, even

when the Rockefeller Foundation proposed to finance a post-graduate medical school in 1927, the offer was ignored, and the money went instead to found the Postgraduate School of Medicine at the Hammersmith Hospital in London.

The idea of setting up a medical school at Oxford also occurred to

Archibald Garrod

Sir Hugh Cairns in 1935 when he returned from a trip to the USA, although Lord Nuffield did say that William Osler had spoken to him in the same vein. At that time Cairns was Head of the Department of Neurosurgery at the London Hospital. On his return he sent a three page letter to Sir Farquhar Buzzard, the Regius Professor of Medicine in Oxford, with a proposal to establish a School of Medicine in Oxford – he suggested it should be small, consisting of no more than 20 students picked from the high flyers of the pre-clinical school in Oxford and also from other medical schools. They would serve three years of clinical training followed by six to eight years of training residences.

Cairns also suggested a collaboration between Professor Howard Florey, an Australian pharmacologist and pathologist who was head of the Sir William Dunn School of Pathology in South Parks Road, and the Nuffield Institute for Medical Research. The latter was now situated at the Radcliffe Observatory, having been purchased by Lord Nuffield in 1929 for the hospital. Its architecture ruled out any prospect of turning it into hospital wards, since, as Dr Cooke, Consultant Physician and Fellow of Merton College, had told everyone, it had no lifts, low water pressure and no temperature regulation.

Medical research had been undertaken in Oxford, notably under Howard Florey since his arrival in 1935. Under his leadership, a team of researchers at the Sir William Dunn School were experimenting on penicillin and showed the effectiveness of it in mice. On 12th February 1941, the first dose of penicillin was given intravenously to a man at the Radcliffe Infirmary. Due to the short supply of the drug it was recycled from the patient's urine by Dr Norman Heatley,[8] a key member of the team involved in the work. He used to cycle back from the Infirmary to the Sir William Dunn school to re-purify it.

---

8 See Cranston D, Sidebottom E, *Penicillin and the Legacy of Norman Heatley.* Words by Design, 2016.

The author David Cranston with Norman Heatley

In 1945 Alexander Fleming, Howard Florey and Ernst Chain were awarded the Nobel Prize in Medicine or Physiology for their "Discovery of penicillin and its curative effect in various infectious diseases." Norman Heatley, a biochemist, was finally recognised in 1990 by the award of an honorary Oxford Doctor of Medicine degree. It was the first time in 800 years the University had ever awarded it to a non-medic.

Following discussion with Buzzard, Lord Nuffield agreed to fund several professorial chairs. Initially, these were planned in medicine, surgery, obstetrics and gynaecology. However, Nuffield insisted on a fourth chair, a

Plaque at the Infirmary site

41

Professor of Anaesthetics. There were no professors of anaesthetics in the British Empire, and Oxford did not regard it as a subject of sufficient standing or merit, arguing that any competent doctor should be able to give an anaesthetic. Nuffield disagreed, founded on his personal experience as a young man when he had had all his bad teeth removed. The nitrous oxide given by the local dentist did not last very long, Nuffield had horrible nightmares and remembered the feeling of suffocation. He contrasted it with another operation where Robert Macintosh of Guy's Hospital was the anaesthetist. When he regained consciousness he demanded to know when the operation was about to start, after it had already finished!

Nuffield assumed that his request, or rather demand, for a fourth chair in anaesthetics would be automatically accepted, and so he was surprised when Buzzard called on him at home one Sunday afternoon to tell him that, deeply grateful as the University was, a chair in anaesthetics would expose both the University and Nuffield to ridicule. Nuffield thanked Buzzard in a friendly way for pointing this out and Buzzard left, assuming that Nuffield had agreed to drop the anaesthetic chair. Two weeks went by, after which Buzzard telephoned to enquire when the University could announce its medical benefaction, only to be told by Nuffield that, at the last interview, he had understood that the University had declined the offer. It then it became crystal-clear that his offer was for four chairs or none. The University gave in, but Nuffield had not finished.

He insisted on Macintosh being nominated for that chair. Macintosh was taken by surprise – he had a thriving private practice in London and saw little attraction in transferring to academic life in Oxford. However, he did not want to cause a breach between his medical friends and Nuffield, and so it was agreed that he would move to Oxford but could keep his private practice in London.

Nuffield offered the University one-and-a-quarter million pounds for the endowment of a Medical School Trust. Shortly afterwards the Congregation of the University was called to accept the gift and express the gratitude of the University. The Chancellor, Lord Halifax, was there, and it was during that meeting (after the gift had been announced) that, quite out of turn, Nuffield stood up and asked if he might say something. He announced that he decided that one-and-a-quarter million pounds was perhaps not quite enough, and he had decided to increase his donation to two million pounds. This allowed a further chair of Orthopaedic Surgery to be added to the four already agreed, and undoubtedly was the beginning of the modern Medical School at Oxford as it is known today. Nuffield expressed his desire for the future of Oxford medicine in the following way:

> *All I want is for the Medical School to turn out 20 brilliant men a year who would go out and teach others.*

The first five Nuffield Professors were Hugh Cairns, Leslie Witts, Gathorne Girdlestone, Robert Macintosh and John Chassar Moir in surgery, medicine, orthopaedics, anaesthetics and obstetrics and gynaecology respectively.

Hugh Cairns

Leslie Witts

Gathorne Girdlestone

John Chassar Moir

Robert Macintosh

**The first five
Nuffield Professors**

The Radcliffe Observatory as the Nuffield Institute of Medical Research

In 1934 the work of the Observatory finally moved to South Africa and the Institute for Medical Research at the Observatory came into being, described by Terence Ryan as *"the oldest and most unsuitable building ever used as an institute of medical research."* The rooms were excessively lofty with windows designed to accommodate telescopes, and the heating and water supply were archaic.

Henry Acland © Ashmoleum

In fact, some medical research had already been done at the Observatory, for in 1854 pollution, or miasma as it was also known, due to badly managed sewage, led to the Oxford cholera outbreak. Wind force and direction could determine how bad this was and Henry Acland, later to become Regius Professor of Medicine, made a study of it stating that:

> *Mr Johnson, the able and indefatigable Radcliffe Observer was able to provide daily measurements of barometer ... humidity ... force of winds, amount of cloud, ozone readings, and proportion of northerly to southerly winds and easterly to westerly winds. In the*

year 1854 of the cholera epidemic there was "a deficiency in humidity and an excess in weight of the air."

Further discussion between Mr Johnson and Professor Acland led to their agreeing with the discoveries of the physician John Snow[9] in London, that water was a very important transmitter of the disease.

The original aim of the Nuffield Institute was to integrate medical research with the work of the Infirmary and it was encapsulated in two initial research subjects, experimental obstetrics and X-ray cinematography.

Professor Gunn had been Professor of Therapeutics in the University of Oxford since he was first recruited by William Osler, and was appointed the first Director of the Institute. He occupied the Observer's House which was renamed Osler House at the request of Lord Nuffield. Dr Alex Cooke, a physician who became the first Director of Clinical Studies in Oxford, supported the medical students and at his instigation it became the centre for the Osler House Club.

Alfred Barkley, affectionately known as Uncle B, was appointed to the staff of the Institute at the age of 60. He was joined by KJ Franklin, a physiologist who had already recognised the value of cine radiography as a non-invasive tool for the study of various physiological processes, and together they observed the movement of joints and the removal of dust from the airways by ciliary action. However, they were better known for their studies on foetal circulation which was undertaken in collaboration with Sir Joseph Barcroft, Professor of Physiology in the University of Cambridge, who became known as the father of foetal physiology.[10] KJ Franklin applied

---

9 John Snow famously located a cholera outbreak in London in 1854 to a water pump and stopped the outbreak by removing the handle of the pump.

10 For example Barclay, AE, Barcroft, J, Barron, DH, Franklin, KJ and Prichard, MML, 1941. "Studies of the Foetal Circulation and of Certain Changes that Take Place after Birth."

cine radiography to a recently delivered lamb lying by its mother still attached to the placenta and sheep were now the principal experimental subjects – it was this that brought a large number of research workers to Oxford to work with Geoffrey Dawes who was then Director of the Institute. Some of these came from as far afield as the United States and Australia and included John Vane who completed his Doctor of Philosophy (DPhil)[11] in 1953 and went on to win the Nobel Prize for his work on Aspirin in 1982.

As this research was carried out on the first floor of the Observatory, the main problem was how to get the sheep up the steps to the first floor. One trick was to have a plank covered in a woollen blanket at their side pushing the sheep against the wall – apparently they appeared to find this a similar sensation as moving with a flock of sheep and were happy to pursue the directive forces of the plank as it was moved by the attendant of the staircase. Others described how they would lift the sheep onto a mat which was then hauled up to the first floor.

Cine radiography was also a means of recording *in vivo* studies of blood flow and circulation for the first time. Sir Hugh Cairns took great interest in cine radiography as a way of exploring the blood supply to the brain. Joe Smith, who arrived in 1968 and set up the Department of Urology in Oxford, focused on understanding the physiological functions of the bladder, using the original antique library steps (still to be seen today at the top of the

Joe Smith

Tower) for people to climb onto the examination couch, leaking urine as they clambered up and down, until he was

---

11 Oxford is the only University in the world which uses the term of 'DPhil' instead of 'PhD'.

The library steps

told that the steps were antiques and he should find some other, less precious, steps for his subjects!

During the Second World War much of the research was related to war injuries. One of the leaders in the management of the injured, who became the Professor of Orthopaedic Surgery, was Joseph Trueta, following his experience of treating war injuries during the Spanish Civil War. His publications explained renal failure after crush injury, so common in the Blitz of the Second World War.

After the war Gordon Ardran was appointed to assume responsibility for the cine radiography research, becoming one of Britain's most distinguished radiologists and the national adviser on radiation injury, establishing close links with the Harwell Atomic Energy Research Establishment. Many medical students became experimental subjects in the disciplines of respiratory physiology and the management of sleep apnoea.

Joseph Trueta

In the 1960s William (Bill) Lund, Consultant Ear Nose and Throat Surgeon to the Radcliffe Infirmary, looked at movements of the larynx, and vocalist Peter Pears and a London singing tutor were recruited for this study. He also looked at the physiological process of swallowing and described how an experimental subject, also presumably a medical student, was encouraged to drink eight pints of beer at the Royal Oak pub opposite the Radcliffe Infirmary. He was then brought back to drink a ninth pint of beer mixed with radioactive material and hung upside down by his ankles to demonstrate the effectiveness of swallowing and the prevention of reflux!

Bill Lund was also involved in the study of sword swallowing. They discovered a sword swallower at the St Giles Fair and persuaded him to attend the Institute. Everything was set up and the loop film was duly made, only to find it was quite useless. The x-ray camera had been set up from the side and as soon as the performer lifted his hand to place the sword vertically above his mouth, the shoulders and upper arms got in the way. However, the problem was finally solved by summoning an unsuspecting secretary from an adjoining office who was asked to stand on a pile of books behind the subject and insert the sword into his mouth which she did with much fear and trembling. The sword swallower was standing rigid to attention, arms by his side and his head thrown back with perspiration breaking out on his forehead as the secretary gradually pushed the sword down, with the performer giving frantic signals with his head and hands regarding the direction of the sword. The whole procedure was analogous to passing a rigid endoscope, but it was completed without any complications from the point of view of the sword swallower... although the effect it had on the secretary is not recorded.

To protect the cine-films, Gordon Ardran had purchased a projector for £5 from the Walton Street Cinema. Loops of film hung from the top of the staircase together with the long smoked sheets of kymographs from the physiology of circulatory studies of the birth of lambs.

One room in the East Wing of the Observatory was the Director's office. There also a small room used by Dr Maureen Owens for bone studies under the supervision of Dame Janet Vaughan, a world leader in the field of radioactive isotopes. When Janet Vaughan moved to the Churchill Hospital, Gordon Ardran used her room to house a small Cayman alligator in a domestic bath. The Cayman was a subject for a large range of studies on the mechanism of swallowing. Not surprisingly, this gave rise to the apocryphal story that this was simply employed by Ardran to maintain occupancy of the room.

The main entrance of the Observatory was used as a tea and coffee area, where social and research discussions took place around an antique table. At Christmas it was used for the staff party, with a bust of Lord Nuffield dressed appropriately as Santa Claus. The doors from the entrance hall to the garden normally remained closed. The centrepiece of the grand entrance hall was the eighteenth century pedestal table which was later moved to the top floor of the Tower of the Winds but, by the year 2000, this table was deteriorating as a result of too much sun exposure. Nevertheless, it was valued at £90,000 and auctioned – the proceeds from its sale were used to commission the current oak furniture in the dining room. It left the Observatory through a window with the help of large crane hired from the north of England.

The oak furniture in the current dining room

On the 10th of March 1971 the postgraduate medical library of the Radcliffe Infirmary was destroyed by fire. The librarian, Maureen Forest, had recently been appointed to develop co-operation between United Oxford Hospital Libraries and found herself in receipt of a consignment of a quarter of a ton of bound journals from the British Medical Association. They were stored in the top of the Tower of the Winds and Radcliffe Infirmary porters were not pleased to be given the job of carrying them up the spiral staircase! Maureen Forest made large numbers of meringues as a bribe and token of thanks. She also recalls the volumes being stored for two years and, it being a warm August when they were retrieved, there was an exceptional number of dead and dying flies to be disposed of before the volumes could be carried downstairs again!

In one of the side rooms on the first floor, a mezzanine level was created by scaffolding and accessed by a steep ladder. It was used for analysis of samples derived from experiments on the sheep on the lower floor. Water came from a tank at the top of the Tower, but that did not generate sufficient pressure to operate the filter pumps needed for the chemical work, and thus that had to be done in the animal house built to the West of the Observatory which was demolished and now replaced by a residential block known as the Doll Building.

The animal house contained rats, rabbits and guinea pigs, and for a short time a coypu who escaped and destroyed some of the electrical wiring. There was a yard at the back of the building where sheep could be brought in from the University Farm and be held for short periods until about to give birth... and also where a pair of goats stripped all the green paint from the doors.

In addition to the main building there were two small rotundas originally built for housing telescopes. The Eastern Rotunda was later a centre for glass blowing for several hospital departments and continued to be so well into the early years of Green College under the supervision of Phil

The two small rotundas originally built for housing telescopes

Tosh, one time chauffeur to the Nuffield Professor of Anaesthetics, Robert Macintosh. At one time the Western Rotunda housed medical artists Audrey Arnott and Fay McLarty, including their prize-winning dachshunds. For a short period the Western Rotunda was used as a records department and bedrooms for a few of the Infirmary doctors. The Eastern Rotunda is now a music room, and remains today, although the Western one was demolished in 1964 when the Radcliffe Infirmary needed to expand its Gibson pathology laboratories building.[12]

In 1971 the Department of Clinical Biochemistry in the Radcliffe Infirmary was in need of expansion and took over the East wing of the Observatory. Here studies on blood coagulation factors were done by Peter Esnouf, also based in

---

12 Named after Alexander Gibson (1875–1950), Radcliffe Infirmary physician and Professor of Morbid Anatomy, and still *in situ* under that name in 2024 as part of the University's Radcliffe Observatory Quarter.

*Destruction of the
western rotunda*

*The remaining
eastern rotunda*

the Gibson Building with Sir Philip Randle, who in 1975 had moved to Oxford from Bristol to found the Department of Clinical Biochemistry.

In the Observatory, the main room to the right of the main entrance became a seminar room on the first floor. What is now the William Gibson Room was taken over by the Director of Postgraduate Studies. One team run by Martin Vessey occupied the large room on the first floor of the Tower of the Winds and the adjacent small room. Their major cohort study was concerned with all methods of contraception and other aspects of women's health. They had large numbers of filing cabinets which were the primary source of information from the 17,000 female study participants. Gerald Draper was another occupant who was involved in the Oxford childhood cancer study. Nobel Prize winner Professor Hans Krebs once had space in this building after his formal retirement from the University and his honorary status allowed him to take lunch in Green College each day.

The Tower of the Winds was also used by an inveterate smoking statistician and an artist who were banished there from the lower floor. During this time the Observatory roof was opened at the rear, overlooking the gardens, with a set of stairs commencing at the gallery and leading up to an ugly meteorological observation tower outside the main building. Clive Hahn, an anaesthetist who was one of the founding Fellows of Green College, remembers that at the time:

The exact purpose of this hut was unknown to me, but it contained, as we discovered when we obtained the building, a hugely powerful pair of German submarine binoculars which gave an excellent view of the all-female St Anne's College across the road and was much in use by the post-doctoral workers and technicians. The binoculars disappeared soon after – probably confiscated by Richard Doll.

The ugly meteorological observation tower

Clive Hahn also remembers that three anaesthetic technicians who worked in the Observatory, Dickie Salt, Alan Ryder and Tony Thompson, had been told of an underground tunnel from the Observatory, blocked off and possibly filled in around the time of the Second World War. However, the only tunnel that Michael Pirie was ever aware of was an underground passage that connected the Harkness Building with the Witts Lecture theatre in the Infirmary under the roadway.

Green College

Richard Doll

The conception for a new Oxford college, centred around the Radcliffe Observatory, was first proposed by Sir Richard Doll, the Regius Professor of Medicine, and the suggestion was that it would be named Radcliffe College. The original intention was that it should be a college largely, but by no means exclusively, for medical tutors, scientists and students, as many of the older colleges were not particularly interested in clinical medicine. This meant that many clinical teachers entitled to a college Fellowship were unable to obtain one, or any other access to college facilities. When the University Hebdomadal Council agreed to the foundation of a College, along the lines Doll suggested, they established a University Committee, the Radcliffe Committee, to oversee its foundation. It was chaired by the Vice Chancellor and its members included Richard Doll, Lord Bullock who was Master of St Catherine's College, and Jack Lankester, the University Architect. In 1976 the Conferences of Colleges voted in favour of the proposal. The following year The Hebdomadal Council of the University authorised the foundation of Radcliffe

College and agreed to allocate the Observatory and its associated buildings and grounds for the use of the college.

Sir Richard Doll raised £250,000 from the Rhodes Trust, Blackwell publications and the Abraham Educational Trust.[13] In the autumn of 1976 Professor Paul Beeson, Nuffield Professor of Medicine, suggested that Dr Cecil Green of Texas Instruments in the USA might be persuaded to provide financial support and Paul Beeson suggested that his friend, Dr William Gibson, Professor of Medical History at the University of British Columbia, who knew Dr Green well, might contact him with a letter together with the gift of an Ackerman print of the Observatory. William Gibson had done his DPhil in Oxford under Sir Charles Sherington, a Nobel laureate who held the Wayneflete Chair of Physiology at Magdalen College. Gibson was one of the first postgraduate students at the new Clinical School in Oxford in 1939 and he later became Vice Chancellor of Vancouver University and President of the American Osler Society encouraging all members to support Osler's house, the 'Open Arms', at 13 Norham Gardens.

The letter and Ackerman print was duly delivered to Cecil Green, and was met with a favourable response. Today the Gibson Room in the College honours William Gibson's role in the founding of the College, for which he was made a Life Fellow.

Cecil Green was born in Manchester two days after Queen Elizabeth the Queen Mother on 6th August 1900. He emigrated to USA when he was two years old and was in San Francisco during the earthquake of 1906. He was educated at the University of British Columbia and studied electrical engineering at the Massachusetts Institute of Technology. He

---

13 Sir Edward Penley Abraham CBE FRS (1913 –1999) was a biochemist and one of the Oxford team instrumental in developing penicillin and cephalosporin. Howard Florey would not patent penicillin but the USA did so after the production went there during World War II, although Oxford did patent cephalosporin – it was that money which formed the basis of the EP Abraham Trust.

worked for a small exploration company, Geophysical Service Incorporated (GSI), which he and four colleagues subsequently bought from its owner just before the Japanese bombed Pearl Harbour. GSI began to manufacture a broad range of electronics equipment and instruments during World War II, including anti-submarine sonar detectors. In 1951 GSI spun off Texas Instruments Incorporated to pursue the manufacture of a broader range of electronics equipment and instruments, with Dr Green in charge. He died at the age of 102 in California.

When Dr Green and his wife Ida visited Oxford in April 1977, they only stayed for four days at that time but signed a contract for which he agreed to provide £1 million in stages, on condition that the first part of the construction of the college was begun by the end of December 1977. He

Ida and Cecil Green

provided a further donation for the Walton Building and part of the McAlpine Quadrangle. Cecil Green wanted the college to be named the Cecil and Ida Green College but Harold Macmillan, the Chancellor of the University at the time, insisted on a single name – Green or nothing – pointing out that Jesus and Trinity only had a single name! The University accepted this change of name in November 1977, much to the disquiet of some, including the Radcliffe Trustees, although they were eventually pacified by the assurance that the college address would always be Green College at the Radcliffe Observatory, Woodstock Road, Oxford. Cecil Green continued to visit the College after the death of his wife where he liked to be introduced to as many staff and Fellows as possible. At dinner he would mention everyone's name and what he had learned about them.

Richard Doll formed various College committees, all of which he chaired and they met in his home in 13 Norham Gardens. The first meeting of the Governing Body took place in the boardroom of the Radcliffe Infirmary on the 8th of December 1977. In 1979 the minutes on notepaper initially headed 'Radcliffe College' showed that it consisted of 30 Fellows.

After every meeting it was compulsory for the Governing Body to attend a dinner at St Anthony's College, where the College Steward was Gerald Chambers, who later was appointed as the Domestic Bursar of Green College in 1979, and as a Governing Body Fellow in 1992.

Julian Britton recalls the dinners in St Anthony's:

> *I don't know how I became a member of the Governing Body but I was very definitely the junior representative of the potential founding Fellows. I did not speak, just listened – to the most amazing discussions. It was a high powered committee of which to be a member, and the discussions between Lord Bullock and Jack Lankester the University Architect were worthy of the Supreme Court or Parliament and the House of Lords.*

The early Fellows were not all medical. A social scientist, Juliet Cheetham, became the first female Fellow and in January 1981 Richard Doll invited Jeffrey Burley to become a Fellow at the College. He had been a University Lecturer in the Forestry Institute with no college connection and welcomed the opportunity, although it was on the provision that Jeffrey might attract a student to the college. In fact he brought ten students and was involved in forming the Green College Centre for Environment and Development. He became head of Plant Sciences and later a very popular President of the International Union of Forestry Research Organisations (IUFRO), the global forestry body.

Richard Doll also encouraged a healthy sporting competition between the Fellows and the college students, including an annual cricket match at which he was both captain and wicket keeper.

Gordon Stirrat, one of the first Fellows, introduced Medical Ethics into the student curriculum and was helped by David Cook who lectured on ethics at Westminster Teacher Training College in Oxford. Clive Hahn, with the support of Gordon Stirrat, suggested that the College needed a chaplain, but as an atheist Richard Doll was not favourably disposed. However David Cook, who was also ordained, had such a good relationship with Richard Doll that he agreed to appoint David as chaplain, and for several years there were services in the Radcliffe Infirmary Chapel at the beginning and end of each term.

Shortly after David Cook left, John Lennox, a Professor of Mathematics and internationally respected Christian Apologist, was appointed as a Pastoral Advisor in David Cook's place and elected as a Governing Body Fellow.

From the beginning, the Radcliffe Observatory became the central focus of the college. The transformation of the Radcliffe Observatory was undertaken through the Buildings Committee and completed in 1980, so in the Michaelmas term of 1979 and the Hilary term of 1980 a buffet luncheon for college members took place in the Stables Bar. The Governing Body Fellows Elect sacrificed a great deal of personal time in order to establish the new college, as did their wives and partners. The furnishing and decoration of the Observatory was undertaken by Joan Doll in conjunction with Jack Lankester the University surveyor and Green College architect, who also had to turn what was originally the stable yard or back entrance of the Observatory into something worthy of a front quadrangle. His concept was to design the entrance as though one was entering the courtyard of an eighteenth century country house with an estate clock over the archway and the Lankester Quad was

The stable block converted into the entrance and Lankester Quad

Sir Richard and Lady Doll open Green College 1ˢᵗ Sept 1979

named in his honour. On the 1ˢᵗ of September 1979, the gates were opened to the first 30 students and Sir Richard Doll became the first Warden. The Observer's House had 15 rooms and 9 and 10 Bradmore Road were leased from the University for the remainder of the students.

In 1972 Terence Ryan was engaged in micro-angiography research with Gordon Ardran in the Observatory where the kitchens are now situated. Later he was invited to be a Fellow at the College. He was asked to set up the Music Society and the Art and Décor Committee and was involved in setting up the Stables Gallery in College for the opening of an exhibition by the Sussex painter Louis Turpin, organised by the surgeon and artist Emanuel Lee. For 20 years it was booked by artists for two weeks sessions. Terence was also given the job of buying a snooker table, and although he confessed to having no knowledge of the game, he did say that his Great Grandfather chaired the Ooty Club in the Nilgiris in India where snooker was first played in 1875!

In 1989 £10,000 was set aside for the College to purchase silver plate cutlery to equip the Dining Room but Bursar Gerald Chambers arranged it very successfully in the Silver Vaults of London for £2,000. The remaining £8,000 was spent on a competition for silver smiths to make a centrepiece. Rod Kelly from the East of England won it. His eight-sided rose bowl modelled on the Tower of the Winds with all the winds was exhibited in National Exhibitions. It was inscribed:

PRIMO ATRIENSI SOCH GRATISSIMI ITA
INSCRIPSERUNT MCMLXXXIX POST DECEM
ANNOS COLLEGIO DE GREEN NECNON
GIRALDO CHAMBERS

Loosely translated as:

The first arrivals (Fellows) inscribe this with gratitude in 1989
after 10 years of Green College
and also Bursar Gerald Chambers

The eight-sided rose bowl and silver flower stand

A silver flower stand was also made with signs of the zodiac on the top, while others gave candlesticks and several Fellows paid a further £1,000 each for octangle salt and pepper condiments for the tables.

All the early Fellows were kept very busy and dined each Thursday to support Richard Doll who had a significant list of guests – mostly other College heads. Gowns were worn and Peter Jones produced a Latin Grace ,now recorded in the official University book of graces.

Pro hoc cibo et solalidate huius
collegii te Deum laudamus
For this food and for the
fellowship of this college, we
praise Thee, O God.

The first private dinner in the Gibson Room was for Terence Ryan's parents' sixtieth wedding anniversary,

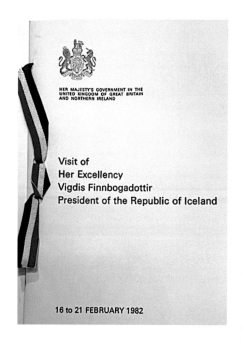

HER MAJESTY'S GOVERNMENT IN THE
UNITED KINGDOM OF GREAT BRITAIN
AND NORTHERN IRELAND

Visit of
Her Excellency
Vigdis Finnbogadottir
President of the Republic of Iceland

16 to 21 FEBRUARY 1982

and on 19th February a buffet luncheon was held for the President of Iceland at the request of the University.

During the 1980s a new building containing student accommodation was built on the site of what had formally been the animal house. It was named somewhat irreverently by the students as 'The Doll's House'! It was not an expensive building and was poorly insulated for noise.

Initially the Walton Building had student accommodation on the ground and first floor, and an underground 100-seat lecture theatre named The Edward Abraham Theatre as the EP Abraham Trust had provided substantial financial support for this. It also included an adjacent office block with guest rooms and a wine cellar. It was converted into a library on the ground floor during Sir David Watson's time as Principal from 2011.

On 13th June 1981 the College was officially opened by the University Chancellor, Harold Macmillan. At the opening, outside in the sun, it appeared that Macmillan was asleep, but it was pretence, for he then gave a memorable speech that slowly and powerfully listed many of the previous donors of Oxford Colleges including Royals and Bishops and, of course, Jesus, Christ Church and Trinity were mentioned to impress Cecil Green and his wife.

When Sir Richard Doll's role as Warden came to an end in 1983, Dr John Trevor Hughes, who was Vice-Warden at the time, did much to secure Sir John Walton as the next warden and was Vice Warden throughout John Walton's seven-year term. John Walton was a well known neurologist who was

*Cecil Green, Harold Macmillan and Richard Doll
at the official opening of Green College*

GREEN COLLEGE
was established 1st September 1979
through the generosity of
Drs. CECIL and IDA GREEN
and was opened by the Chancellor
The Rt. Hon. HAROLD MACMILLAN O.M., F.R.S., D.C.L.
on 13th June 1981

formally Dean of Medicine at Newcastle and President of the General Medical Council, and was created Lord Walton of Detchant while Warden. He amazed the College by knowing everyone's name and occupation, including the students, while seeming to take on more and more national and international presidencies. His wife Betty had a great love of music, was a fine pianist and did much to bring the college Music Society to a high standard. Walton was followed by Sir Crispin Tickell, formally British Ambassador to Mexico and British Ambassador for the United Nations, but he could not come to Oxford for one year until 1990, and thus in 1989 Trevor Hughes became Acting Warden for that year.

Past Wardens of Green College pictured at the 25th Anniversary party:
Dr John Trevor Hughes, Lord Walton of Detchant, Sir Crispin Tickell,
Sir John Hanson, Sir Richard Doll.

During his tenure, Sir Crispin became Oxford University's Principal spokesman on climate change and was also responsible for the creation of the Green College Centre for Policy and Understanding. His primary aim was to establish a forum where the political, environmental, scientific, industrial, business, financial and media worlds could meet the academic world. It was during his tenure as Warden that a link was established with Reuters and the Reuters Fellowship. He also referred to his recent office at the United Nations to give the College a higher national and international profile.

The governing body approved the establishment of an Advisory Council with HRH Princess Anne as one of the first members of the council, meeting annually to advise the Warden and the governing body on emerging issues and future developments. This only lasted during Sir Crispin's tenure. Princess Anne played her role with enthusiasm and entered helpfully into discussions on education. She also opened the Osler McGovern Centre at 13 Norham Gardens. Thursday night

HRH Princess Anne meets some of the students

dinners brought many of Sir Crispin's colleagues to the high table, including Mrs Thatcher, Joanna Lumley and Boutros Boutros-Ghali, the head of the United Nations.

Sir Crispin Tickell's tenure came to an end in 1997 and he was followed by Sir John Hanson (1998-2006) who had previously been Director General of the British Council. During his time it was decided that the medical role of the College would be enhanced by owning the home of the father of modern medicine, Sir William Osler, at 13 Norham Gardens, which had previously been leased – when the lease expired, the College purchased it from the University. Margaret Hanson was a much loved Warden's wife who sadly fell ill and died during his time as Warden. Sir John Hanson increased the academic strength of the college with the appointment of several new Fellows and a large increase in student numbers. He also enhanced international connections, fostering links with overseas foundations in New Zealand and the United States and, together with Dr John Wass, he was instrumental in securing the Kawasaki Research Fellowship scheme with Kawasaki University in Japan for the College.

The student body increased in diversity during his tenure, with 42 different nationalities present among the students in 2003. He initiated external conservation work on the Observatory and the work was recognised in 2005 with the Oxford Preservation Trust's most prestigious award.

Sir John Hanson also supported Charles Barclay, former director of the Blackett Observatory at Marlborough College and past Vice President of the Royal Astronomical Society, in raising the profile of the Radcliffe Observatory's history, by launching the Astronomy for All Lecture Series, an event which continues to take place every year.

A mission statement of the college was established in 1999 to take it into the new millennium:

> *The mission of Green College is to provide academic, administrative and social support for Fellows, students, common room members and academic visitors working in pure and applied subjects related to human health and welfare.*

It was John Hanson with Michael Earl, the Dean of Templeton, who together initiated the process of the merger of Green College with Templeton College. The Fellows of both governing bodies moved gradually, from concerns and reservations about a merger, to a near consensus in favour. It was brought to successful fruition in 2008 by John Hanson's successor Colin Bundy, a South African historian and former Director of the School of Oriental and African Studies, who took over as Warden in 2006 and became the first Principal of Green Templeton College. He described the College's embrace of the merger as *"truly innovative, imaginative and courageous: the first merger of Oxford colleges since the sixteenth century."*

Chris Bulstrode (1951-2023) was another student who later became a Fellow of the College. Well known for his student pranks, on one April Fool's Day he spotted that by adjusting just one sign he could create a circular one-way traffic system around Oxford which ended in a continuous loop. He had that knack of spotting the absurd and could not resist the temptation! When the police found out who was responsible, Dr Jim Holt, the Director of Clinical Studies at the time, called Chris into his office and is reputed to have said:

> *In five minutes the police will come in through that door. I suggest you leave by the back door and disappear for three weeks.*

On another occasion a noticeable set of large, black cardboard footprints appeared striding up, over and down the Tower of the Winds. In a judgement of Solomon, another Director of Clinical Studies, Dr Michael Dunhill, summoned Chris and said:

> *Some wretched person has defaced the Tower of the Winds. I don't know who the idiot was, but I do know that you are the only person who can get them down, so please would you oblige?*

In the Autumn of 2019 the 40th anniversary of Green College was celebrated which included a Son et Lumiére and a series of talks by Senior Fellows on the Sunday which was the last day of the celebrations.

TEMPLETON COLLEGE

Historically British universities did not consider Business Studies a worthy subject to be taught at their institutions, and at Oxford the famous Warden of New College, Dr Spooner, in the early years of the twentieth century, summed up the feeling of the academic community to this, denouncing:

> *Too much of the brains and vigour of the country being attracted towards the wealth amassing career of commerce or business to the neglect of the more ennobling careers of the clergyman, the lawyer, the doctor, and even the public servant.*[14]

Indeed, the view of many businessmen was similar. William Morris (Lord Nuffield) was completely self taught, learning from trade journals and engineering manuals. He never regarded formal high-level training as being of any great value for his business career or those of his executives, saying:

> *I have lived long enough to know that it is not always the men who have an expensive education who do things.*

It was not until after the Second World War that a more academic approach to business studies rose on the University

---

14 Arena, L and Dang, RJ, 2010, July. "Learning lessons from the past: A historical exploration of a century of business education at Oxford and Cambridge (1900s-2000s)," in *Management History Research Group Conference.*

agenda when, in both the United States and the UK, an increasing number of businessmen started questioning why business should remain a profession which needed no academic training and was considered to be on a lower level than medicine or engineering. In 1949, Oxford welcomed the annual Conference of the Federation of British Industry, which gathered representatives of industry and the University, paving the way for the creation of a more formal training in business within the University context. In 1953 there had been the first Oxford University Business Summer School for 40 to 50 young men in industry, taking place at Worcester College, where the lectures involved both macroeconomics (labour economics and government issues) and microeconomics (the theory of the firm and of industries). While the Summer School was not officially recognised as part of Oxford University, it did forge initial bonds between the University and the business world.

In the early 1960s Lord Franks, who was then Provost of Worcester College, first thought about the possibility of establishing a Business School in Oxford and Cambridge, although at that stage the Vice Chancellor made it clear that Oxford University was not in favour.[15]

The following year, an American Educational Trust linked to the McKinsey management consultancy firm helped to fund a report on the possibility of developing management education in Oxford. As a result of this, the Board of the Faculty of Social Studies in Oxford agreed to form a special committee on Management Education. This led to a favourable response from the University and allowed John Wright, a Fellow of Trinity College, Oxford, a sabbatical for one term to visit the United States and to write a report on Business Education in Oxford. He concluded that, if Management Studies was going to be introduced in Oxford, it must bear some useful relation to the existing studies.

---

15 A more detailed account can be found in Graves, D, *Templeton College: The First Thirty Years*, 2001.

The three influential Oxford Fellows who conceived and created the Oxford Centre for Management Studies (OCMS) were Norman Leyland, then investment bursar at Brasenose College, George Richardson of St John's College and later Warden of Keble College, subsequently running Oxford University Press, and John Wright. They were all economists who ran a course for business executives at the Oxford Business Summer School. In 1960 Philip Shelbourne, a tax barrister who was a regular speaker at the summer school, asked George Richardson if he might bring along to an evening seminar a friend and client called Clifford Barclay, a tax accountant and entrepreneur who had already made his fortune at 50, and who decided he would like to do something to help establish Business Studies at Oxford.

Clifford Barclay sculpture

Clifford Barclay's parents had emigrated from Poland at the turn of the century and Clifford was born in 1907 in England. He left school at 16 and enrolled as an articled clerk in a firm of chartered accountants, Stoy Hayward. He was made partner at 23. By the time he left in 1955 as a senior partner, the firm had been recognised throughout the UK in the sphere of tax advice. A sculpture of him now sits in the Fellows Study at Green Templeton College.

As a result of attending this seminar, Clifford Barclay agreed to provide the start-up funding needed for the birth of OCMS. The first four programmes were run from 161 Woodstock Road, with members staying in the Randolph Hotel.

Norman Leyland, Bursar of Brasenose College, was the founding director and Norman (later Sir Norman) Chester, Warden of Nuffield College, was the founder chairman. The Committee, under the chairmanship of Norman Chester, recommended an institution completely independent of University control, free to experiment while both drawing on, and contributing to, University resources.

Thus, in 1965, OCMS was formed as an 'associated institution' of the University and began to run a six-month course for general managers and custom-built courses for specific companies.

By this time there were some management orientated courses for undergraduates and a few University students had enrolled for a DPhil in Management Studies. The OCMS trustees included Sir John Davis of the Rank Organization, Hugh Parker of McKinsey, Sir Ronald Leach of Peat Marwick Mitchell, David Sieff of Marks and Spencer and Ashley Raeburn of Shell, as well as Clifford Barclay.

OCMS subsequently moved to a newly built complex in an 18.7 acre site in Kennington on land bought from St John's College for £14,500, designed by Richard Burton of Burton Ahrend and Jellinek. The bedrooms were designed by John Makepeace the wellknown furniture designer. The new modernist building was opened officially by HRH The Duke of Edinburgh in 1969.

Norman Leyland retired as Director to be replaced by Bob Tricker in 1971. Sadly Norman Leyland died in an accident, falling off his bicycle in 1981 on his way home from teaching at Kennington – he was only 60 years old.

In 1980 Dr Uwe Kitzinger was appointed as Director. He had been deputy warden of Nuffield College but at the time was in leadership at Institut Européen d'Administration des Affaires (INSEAD) Business School in France. He argued for the creation of a Faculty of Management, which was not dominated by the Faculty of Economics, stating that *"the*

Norman Chester, Norman Leyland, HRH The Duke of Edinburgh and
Clifford Barclay at the opening of Oxford Centre for Management Studies in 1969

Templeton College

Management Centre needed to be transformed into a College." At this stage, OCMS was struggling financially, and one way that Kitzinger found to raise funds was to give lectures on cruises. It was not really his scene, as he preferred sailing his own boat, and this attempt at fund raising did not always go smoothly. On one cruise at which Uwe was a guest speaker, a traveller from the United States who disagreed strongly with him suggested Uwe be thrown overboard for his comments!

However, he managed to persuade the editor of the American Oxonian, the magazine of North American Rhodes Scholars Alumni, to publish an article entitled 'A College in Search of a Founder'. As a result of this, John Templeton contacted Uwe Kitzinger to offer his assistance.

John Templeton was born in 1912, in Winchester, Tennessee. His parents encouraged an entrepreneurial spirit. An exceptional student, he obtained a scholarship to Yale University, and then a Rhodes scholarship to Oxford where he obtained an MA in Law. As a result of many shrewd investments, he became a very wealthy banker and

John Templeton

Judith Folk

philanthropist. In 1999 Money Magazine called him, *"the greatest Global stock picker of the century."* He married Judith Folk in 1937 and, following her death in a motorcycle accident, married Irene Reynolds Butler. She died in 1993, by which time he had renounced his United States citizenship and held dual Bahamian and British citizenship and was living in the Bahamas where he later died in 2008.

John Templeton offered five million dollars towards the College on four conditions, including requirements for matriculation rights and the seeking of a Royal Charter, which would have made the institution into an independent College of Oxford University.

In 1984, the University agreed on the matriculation rights but did no more at that stage than "to note the Royal Charter ambition". However, as a result of this Templeton College was founded, named after John Templeton's parents, and Uwe Kitzinger became President of the College.

The 1980s saw huge growth in the range of Templeton College activities. Its income grew from £720,000 to £4,000,000,

Norman Chester, Sir John and Lady Templeton and Uwe Kitzinger at the Templeton College naming ceremony in 1984

its executive education expanded, and its reputation for research flourished, not least through the creation of four research centres in Information Management, Retail Management, Employee Relations and Major Project Management. Other activities included 'Oxford Economics', now a global economic consultancy headed by John Walker, and 'Fast Track' which Hamish Stevenson started and, as it developed and expanded, became independent.

Meanwhile the College and the University grew closer and programmes were run for a number of organisations including the Greater London Council, Barclays Bank, Thames Water and the Peninsular and Oriental Steam Navigation Company.

In 1981 all College Fellows became members of the Social Studies Faculty and by 1987 the College was recognised as a 'society of entitlement', a step on the path to full college status, supervising many more students studying for DPhil, MPhil and MLitt programmes, although 1978 had been the year of the first conferment of a DPhil in Management Studies.

In 1988, the University's Moser Committee, appointed to look into the future development of Management Studies at Oxford, recommended that a new school of Management Studies be established on the Kennington site incorporated with Templeton College. Founded as the University's School of Management Studies in 1992, it taught an MBA[16] degree and an extended range of joint undergraduate degrees involving management. A new business school posed challenges for Templeton College as a continuing entity. The College would lose its graduate and undergraduate programmes, important funding, and its hard-earned identity, unless a new role and funding regime were carved out.

After much discussion, it was agreed that Templeton would get full College status under a Royal Charter and retain its executive education activities, whilst working alongside a

16 Master of Business Administration.

new business school handling all undergraduate and graduate programmes. Templeton received a Royal Charter on 23rd May 1995 and on 31st July, 30 years after its foundation, the name was changed to Templeton College (OCMS). Responsibility for the College now rested with the Governing Body Fellows which included five non-academic Fellows to be known as Barclay Fellows.

In 1995 the College was supported by a further donation of £3.2 million towards its endowment by John Templeton.

After Uwe Kitzinger there were a number of Directors including Dr Michael von Clemm (an American businessman, restaurateur and anthropologist) and Dr Clark Brundin (an American-born academic who had been Vice Chancellor of the University of Warwick). In 1998 Brundin was succeeded by Sir David Rowland who had been Chairman of Lloyd's between 1993 and 1997 and had been responsible for safeguarding the future of the Lloyd's market through a very difficult period.

SAÏD BUSINESS SCHOOL

Wafic Saïd

In 1996, after three years of discussions, the Syrian-born businessman Wafic Saïd put up the first £20 million for a Business School, on condition that the University would obtain a matching £20 million from other benefactors. At that stage, the biggest donation was from Lord Sainsbury who gave his name to the Saïd Business School Library. John Kay, an economist who had been Director of The Institute of Fiscal Studies, was then invited to become the first Director of the Saïd Business School.

In 1998 the Oxford City Council granted planning permission for the Business School to be located opposite Oxford Railway Station. John Kay resigned suddenly in 1999, feeling that his efforts to help Oxford adapt to a new environment were being rebuffed. Anthony Hopwood, a British accounting academic, who had been Professor of International Accounting and Financial Management at the London School of Economics, succeeded John Kay as the new Director of the School in 1999. He died in 2010 and according to his Obituary in the *Guardian*, he was fond of saying that

"business is so interesting, and most business schools are so boring"
His vision was for an 'intelligent' business school.

On 5th November 2001, the Saïd Business School building opened – designed by Jeremy Dixon and Edward Jones, architects of the Royal Opera House conversion and the extension of the National Portrait Gallery.

While the University's School of Management Studies was running an MBA programme and the existing joint degrees in management, Templeton retained responsibility for executive education until 2002 when Oxford Executive Education was launched by the University to further develop executive education at Oxford. This was a collaboration between the College and Saïd Business School, pooling their strengths, resources and experience.

Building on its role as Oxford's specialist graduate College in Management Studies, Templeton had become the centre of a high-level network, bringing together Fellows, students and alumni, business leaders, and leaders of thought to cross-fertilise study and debate, and to catalyse new approaches.

Much of its research was focused in specialist centres which grew out of earlier initiatives and explored key issues and pioneered understanding of critical issues confronting the international business community. Centres included: the Oxford Institute for Employee Relations (OXIFER); the Oxford Healthcare Management Institute (OHCMI); the Oxford Institute of Information Management (OXIIM); the Oxford Institute of Retail Management (OXIRM); and the Oxford Institute of Strategic and International Management (OXISIM).

The College also hosted the Emerging Markets Forum, the Oxford Futures Forum, the Oxford Chairs and Chief Executive Officers' Dinner Discussions, the NHS Chairs Group, and the Tomorrow Project, a confidential suicide prevention service set up to provide both suicide crisis and bereavement support in response to the needs and concerns of local communities. Information technology played an important role in bridging management, government, and the public sector – the pre-office training of the Labour Shadow Cabinet had been undertaken by the College in 1996 and many Fellows were involved in a range of projects, from change management in government departments to studies of changing public sector roles. Rosemary Stewart was one of the first group of Fellows recruited by OCMS and she, together with Sue Dopson and others, had a major involvement with the NHS, including the evaluation of projects aimed at improving clinical effectiveness, and looking at pathways to facilitate moving the results of medical research into clinical practice.

In 2002, Professor Michael Earl took over as Dean of Templeton, which retained responsibility for executive education. He had previously been a lecturer in Management at the Manchester Business School before coming to Oxford in 1976 as a Fellow at Templeton College and founding Director of the Oxford Institute of Information Management. He then spent eleven years at the London Business School, and in 2002 he became Dean of Templeton College and Professor of Information Management in the University of Oxford.

A major restructuring of the College and the School, initiated by the Dean of the Saïd Business School, Professor Anthony Hopwood, and the Dean of Templeton, was facilitated by the fact that they knew each other well, having been colleagues previously. As a result, responsibility for all Management Studies teaching, both undergraduate, postgraduate and executive, was consolidated within the Saïd Business School in 2005.

At the time of the transfer of the teaching of executive education to the Saïd Business School, the University agreed a sum of £20m for the goodwill and ownership of Egrove, the Kennington site, for which Templeton College received a rent-free lease. The £20m was made up of the ownership of two freehold buildings, King Charles House, an office building, and a residential building near the Saïd Business School. This move and the accompanying resources allowed Templeton to develop its role as a graduate college. Following this, a meeting took place to consider the alternative scenarios available to Templeton College, chaired by Michael Earl and led by Keith Ruddle. These included a merger with another College, and so discussions were had with four Oxford colleges. Green College was chosen on the basis of it being of a similar vintage and a postgraduate college with a complementary outlook. Negotiations took place over a two-year period and as a result, in 2008, Green College and Templeton College merged to become Green Templeton College. Subsequently Templeton College moved from Kennington to the Woodstock Road site, near to where OCMS had begun. Thus, a small acorn planted in 1965 had grown into two large oak trees – Green Templeton College and the Saïd Business School.

It is undeniable that there will continue to be massive changes in management and Management Studies as research approaches are confronted with new questions. Over the last 40 years there has been a rise of globalisation and with it the need for greater cultural understanding. The accelerating pace of technological advance, especially in information technology with the increasing speed of communications has had its knock-on effects on organisational and managerial decisions. Above all is the relentless pressure to innovate and keep one step ahead of the competition.

Another common theme is the decline of large corporate solutions imposed from above in favour of smaller scale more agile and entrepreneurial ground-up approaches. This downsizing, the collapsing of hierarchies, and the flattening of organisational pyramids, outsourcing, sharing, and reliance on a sophisticated mesh of supply chains will bring new opportunities, including the need to engage with individual employees to unlock their untapped potential, together with the need for corporations to enter into a more open and constructive dialogue with wider society.

One danger that needs to be avoided in Management Studies is building theoretical frameworks without a concern for the practical applications. Academics and reflective practitioners need to work alongside one another in communities that produce high-quality, relevant focused insights in the tradition of grounded research. There is a strong case for maintaining this combined scholar and practitioner research team approach on the ground, and if knowledge can be co-produced and combined in novel ways, the results could produce the dazzling synthesis that could profoundly advance management theory, teaching, and practice. Templeton College has thrived from the mixture of academic and practitioner worlds and that continues in Green Templeton College.

And finally, perhaps one future area for management study could be the University of Oxford itself, as Keith Ruddle once reflected:

> *Consider Oxford University and its 'family' – a complex amalgam of academics, students, staff, colleges, departments, institutes, collaborations, and partnerships. Governance is diffuse, often characterised as hopelessly bureaucratic and cumbersome. Any major change on decision involves democratic consensus to an extreme degree. Detractors say we need more top-down management. But, inspite of this, Oxford achieves change, pursues radically new research, and continues to educate the political, academic, and business leaders of the future. It has survived revolution and religious strife and has done so for nearly 900 years, maybe we should study more closely how its loose connections work in action.*[17]

---

17 Dopson, S, Earl, M, Snow, P (eds), *Mapping the Management Journey*. OUP.

Green Templeton College

Green Templeton College was established in its current form in October 2008 through the merger of Green and Templeton Colleges. Green College occupied the site, but it had no Royal Charter so was not independent of the University. Templeton brought with it the Royal Charter, as a result of which the University gave the site to Green Templeton College and responsibility of the College then rested with the Governing Body Fellows.

The Warden of Green College at the time of the merger was Professor Colin Bundy, and Michael Earl was the Dean of Templeton College.

Lord Patten, Colin Bundy, Dr John Templeton, Michael Earl, John Hood at the Green Templeton Founders' Dinner, 24th September 2008

Founding Fathers of Green Templeton College

Clifford Barclay

Norman Chester

Richard Doll

Cecil Green

Norman Leyland

John Templeton

After a vote of the Governing Bodies of both colleges, Colin Bundy became head of the newly formed Green Templeton College and the name of the post was changed from Warden to Principal. Sir David Watson succeeded him. He was previously Vice Chancellor of Brighton University (1990-2005) and Professor of Higher Education Management at the Institute of Education (2005-2010). Both a Choral Exhibitioner at Cambridge University and a fine pianist, David shared his passion for music with staff and students. He and his wife Betty held regular musical soirees in the Principal's Lodgings to encourage any musical College member of any standard to perform.

Professor Ingrid Lunt became acting Principal following Sir David Watson's premature death in February 2015, and remained in place until the arrival of Professor Denise Lievesley, formerly Chief Executive of the English Information Centre for Health and Social Care and Director of Statistics at UNESCO. She arrived in 2015 to find a College still in mourning for David Watson's untimely death. However, she was delighted to follow in the footsteps of Sir Richard Doll as a fellow member of the Statistical Dining Club, and worked to support the Reuters Institute, which she described as *a jewel in the Green Templeton crown. Especially nowadays given our concerns about trustworthiness of the media and politicians.* Her partner, Professor Roland Rosner, initiated some informal concerts which included singers, piano players, dancers and poets, and he was responsible for organising family get-togethers for those Green Templeton College students who had children.

Denise was succeeded in 2020 by Sir Michael Dixon, formerly Director of the Natural History Museum in London, who had to manage the transition in a college, like the rest of the world in lockdown, due to the Covid virus.

While the site of the College has not moved since Green College was founded in 1979, the administrative centre of the University is due to move from Wellington Square to the old

David Watson

Ingrid Lunt

Denise Lievesley

View from the college lawn

Dr John Radcliffe looking very pleased with what his benefaction has created

Infirmary site with the Radcliffe Observatory as the focal point of the newly developed Radcliffe Quarter. The Stephen A Schwarzman Centre for the Humanities next door will not only house philosophy and theology, but also has a large concert hall beneath the main building and some facilities which are open to the general public. In due course, it will restore the Radcliffe Observatory building as a social and learning hub, housing a world-class library environment and offering meeting spaces in the wings. It will again make possible the utilisation of the grand South entrance, which at present feels slightly cut off from the college grounds. It provides the setting for the main façade of the building and is becoming significant as the focal point of the Radcliffe Observatory Quarter, complete with the sculpture of Dr John Radcliffe looking very pleased with what his benefaction has created.

Today the College brings together nearly 700 students and over 300 academics and practitioners. While it retains a strong focus on medicine and health, it is now the University of Oxford's pre-eminent graduate college for Management Studies, with many Fellows holding faculty posts at Saïd Business School.

Its mission, as stated in its Royal Charter, is to further postgraduate study and research within the University alongside a college that enables all Members and Fellows to deliver on their potential and thrive throughout life.

The Observatory lit up to welcome the new intake of students in October 2024

The College Gardens

Michael Pirie

Green College inherited two existing gardeners who had worked on the Observatory site long before the time of the College's establishment in 1979. Both of them retired shortly after Michael Pirie's appointment. Michael is an intellectual gardener of whom the college is proud, who also has an extensive knowledge of the history of the College. For many years he has been responsible for maintaining the gardens of the College in such a way as to be suitable for all users of the College, although the main objective of the garden is to be aesthetically pleasing.

When the observatory was built in the late eighteenth century, the surrounding gardens were reminiscent of a landscape park around a small country house and were valued as an exquisite amenity to the observer ensuring unimpeded views all around. In due course some of the land was acquired by the Infirmary to allow for its expansion. While the eighteenth century was a largely a time for identification and classification of plants, the nineteenth century brought the public into closer contact with them. Today the beautifully maintained gardens by Michael and his assistant Carolyn Serra are a delight to all members of the

Radcliffe Observatory, 1810
© MMA / The Elisha Whittelsey Collection / Science Source

College flower borders

College. They provided a beautiful floral design of the College's crest and a celebration of the Transit of Venus in 2012. Their effort in getting the gardens straight after marquees damage the lawn, and maintaining the stunning trees and flower beds, are greatly appreciated. Michael is also responsible for developing the medicinal herb garden with a well annotated description which was prepared by him, Dr Jeffrey Aronson and Professor Elisabeth Hsu (see Appendix 1).

The medicinal herb garden

The college crest in flowers

The transit of Venus

THE GREEN TEMPLETON SUNDIAL

The Green Templeton College Sundial is situated in the Lankester Quad on the right as one enters the college. It commemorates the bi-centenary of the Radcliffe Observatory, and was unveiled at Green College on 21st June 1995, the summer solstice, by the Warden of the College at the time, Sir Crispin Tickell.

It was designed by the Greenwich Observatory and created by the Sculptor Martin Jennings, a Fellow of the Royal Society of Sculptors, who was also responsible for the bronze statue of Dr John Radcliffe on the south lawn. The Sundial is described as a vertical, declining, noon-mark and mean-time dial, which is explained more fully in Appendix 2.

THE COAT OF ARMS

In September 2007, the Royal College of Arms was asked to design a new coat of arms for Green Templeton College. It combines aspects of both Green and Templeton's coats of arms, and its symbolic heraldry captures the spirit of each of their histories and character and current mission. The shield incorporates the Rod of Asclepius and the Nautilus shell. The serpent coiled around a staff is a symbol for the healing arts. Asclepius, the son of Apollo, was a practitioner of medicine in Greek mythology and was at the centre of the coat of arms of Green College.

The Nautilus shell, which symbolises evolution and renewal, was chosen by Sir John Templeton and adopted by Templeton College in 1984 when it changed its name from the Oxford Centre for Management Studies.

In the full coat of arms, there is a crest featuring a heraldic representation of the sun behind the astronomical symbol for Venus (♀) paying homage to the historically important transit of Venus across the sun in 1761. It was the lack of appropriate facilities to observe this cosmological event in Britain that led to the building of the Radcliffe Observatory.

13 Norham Gardens by Valerie Petts

13 Norham Gardens

Situated in the centre of Oxford next to the University Parks, the beautiful Grade II listed Victorian building of 13 Norham Gardens is now owned by Green Templeton College. It is known to the medical community throughout the world as the Oxford home of William and Grace Osler. It was built on woodland and farm land first owned by Henry VIII's physician who delivered Edward VI from Jane Seymour, and later on the land was purchased by St John's College. The house was designed and built by the architect of the Randoph Hotel, William Wilkinson, in the nineteenth century for the Public Orator – it is included in a celebrated book on the architecture of the time. In 1888 it was the birthplace of Sir John Conybeare, London's distinguished physician and outside assessor to the founding of Oxford's Clinical Medical School.

William and Grace Osler arrived in Oxford in 1905 and bought 13 Norham Gardens, moving in in 1907 after refurbishments. William Osler was a Canadian physician who moved to the United States to become one of the founding fathers of Johns Hopkins Hospital in Baltimore. He became the most famous physician of his day and was in great demand for his expertise. His wife was delighted when he was offered the Regius Chair of Medicine in Oxford at the age of 55, as she was worried by how exhausted he was becoming in the United States.

Under William and Grace's ownership it became known as 'The Open Arms' due to its renowned hospitality as a meeting place and source of inspiration for medical students, physicians, scientists and academic visitors as well senior United States military personnel during and after the First World War.

After the sad death of their only surviving son at Ypres in 1917, Osler left the house to his wife, expressing the wish that, on her death, the house be given to Christ Church, of which he was a student,[18] as were all the Regius Professors of Medicine in Oxford.

Farquhar Buzzard, Regius Professor of Medicine in 1928 at the time of Grace Osler's death, did not want to occupy the house, and Christ Church let it to other tenants. During the Second World War it was used as home to part of the Mathematical Institute and as a hostel for the 'Society of Home Students' which later became St Anne's College. It also hosted the Moot discussion club that included notable intellectuals such as TS Eliot. In 1953 Christ Church conveyed the property to the University to be held on trust and Sir George and Caroline Pickering took over the tenancy in apartments there when he became Regius Professor of Medicine in 1956. In 1968, he was succeeded by Sir Richard Doll who lived there with his wife Joan until 1979. His successor, Professor Sir Henry Harris, did not wish to live there and in 1982 it was leased to Green College for 21 years on condition that a quarter of the gross income received by the college for lettings and accommodation would be paid to the Osler Trust, to be part of the cost of the Regius Professor's stipend. Lord Walton and his wife, Betty, were the last couple to live there and it was agreed that the University Newcomers Club could occupy part of the premises on a sub-lease.

When Sir John Hanson became Warden of Green College, he was able to purchase 13 Norham Gardens from the University with the help of generous contributions from foundations and friends, including the Alexander Patrick

---

18 Fellows at Christ Church are known as students.

Linacre, Harvey and Sydenham on the mantelpiece at Norham Gardens

Foundation and Dr John McGovern of Galveston Texas. The latter founded the American Osler Society and over many years he also provided funding for its maintenance and re-design for residents.

While the majority of Osler's extensive library was left to his *alma mater* McGill University, 13 Norham Gardens still has a number of Osler's books and letters and items of furniture, including the famous portraits of Linacre, Harvey and Sydenham that William Osler first saw in Henry Acland's library and of which Grace Osler arranged for a copy to be made for William as a birthday present.

Several letters of great interest are in the collection, including a copy of the letter the Prime Minister, Arthur Balfour, wrote inviting Osler, on behalf of the King, to the Regius Chair in Oxford.

Although the library is primarily a celebration of Osler's life and work, it is also home to various other medical collections, including those of Sir Richard Doll and his work linking lung cancer to smoking. It also houses the story of penicillin and the role of the Oxford Team in its production with one of the original 'penicillin Doulton Ware culture pans'

Confidential
Dictated
My dear Sir
I have the permission of the King to propose to you the appointment to the vacant Chair of Medicine in the University of Oxford. I am satisfied that your selection will command the formal approval of the University and of all those interested in the advancement of Medical science and I sincerely trust that you will find yourself able to give a favourable reply to this invitation which I have the honour to address to you
I am sir, Yours Sincerely
Arthur James Balfour

The letter the Prime Minister, Arthur Balfour, wrote inviting Osler, on behalf of the King, to the Regius Chair in Oxford

on display. The house is a Custodian of the History of the Radcliffe Infirmary and has an extensive literature on leprosy, on which the World Health Organisation based their website. It also has Oxford's largest collection on Traditional, Alternative and Complementary Medicine literature.

Today, 13 Norham Gardens is home to the Osler-McGovern Centre, which promotes the integration of the art and science of medicine by uniting a community of scholars through programmes including lectures, seminars, workshops, conferences, visiting scholars and post-doctoral fellows. It is also home to the Reuters Institute for the Study of Journalism, which engages newsroom leaders from around the world and explores the future of global journalism.

The Osler House Battles

When Lord Nuffield purchased the Radcliffe Observatory for the Medical School in the 1930s the original Observer's House was taken over to provide space for the administrative offices of the medical school and to provide rooms for a joint social club and small library for clinical students. Nuffield insisted that the Observer's House should now be called Osler House after William Osler who Nuffield (then William Morris) had known very well and had become a personal friend before Osler's death in 1919. The Oslers had owned a motor car and although it was not a form of transport in which Osler's wife, Grace, took great pleasure, it did make it easy to reach otherwise inaccessible places, and occasionally the Oslers used it for longer trips. When the car would not start one day and an important rural consultation was jeopardised, their chauffeur recommended *"a young Oxford mechanic by the name of William Morris"* who then worked through the night to repair the cracked cylinder head. Morris became the family mechanic and whenever the car would not start, the cry would go up from Osler, *"Send for Willy."* In turn Osler became William's physician when he suffered from various ailments. On one occasion, after listening to his medical history, Osler struck Morris a sharp blow in the stomach and told him he had a peptic ulcer which he fully deserved from his lifestyle, saying he was *"bloody lucky"* it had not perforated. William Morris would also insist that no doctor was worth consulting who did not have Osler's classic book on his shelves, *The Principles and Practice of Medicine,* and he wanted to name a building at the Radcliffe Infirmary after him. It was almost certainly partly in memory of Osler that many of Morris' later medical benefactions were made.

The Osler Club was eventually recognised as an official University club for medical students in 1948 and they enjoyed the facilities in the now renamed Observer's House that Nuffield had purchased. It shared the premises and the adjacent stables with the Medical School offices. The garden became well used, a squash court was built and tennis courts upgraded. The bar with Mr Launchbury as barman was at its centre, and it became host to outsiders, especially at lunch when Dr Vollum, the bacteriologist, would bring in friends, and junior doctors from the Radcliffe Infirmary would often visit. Foreign visitors from Europe and the Commonwealth were also welcome. Nurses as girlfriends were banned, but Annual Balls were hosted by Matron at the Randolph Hotel. The adjacent stables became a lecture theatre and in November and December the yearly Tingewick Pantomime was rehearsed and scenery painted and the final night party held.[19]

These were the days when at times the yearly intake was very low. In the early days there were two intakes a year – Terence Ryan's year of 1956 consisted of an intake of only eight students with a further small intake later that year, but only one woman. It could be difficult to produce a pantomime and form a rugby team with such small numbers. Terence Ryan acted in three pantomimes, directing one in the year George Pickering was appointed as Regius Professor. He was the first Regius Professor to have research beds and in the pantomime that year was depicted as a villain. Five students were fined by Pickering after the yearly Christmas rag got out of control but a kindly surgeon, Ted Maloney, picked up the bill.

---

19 The Pantomine still occurs, but the spelling of Tingewick has to be different every year!

However, on 26th July, 1978 Osler House was finally closed to the Clinical School. It was described by the students of the day as 'The Great Eviction'. Dr Lyn Williamson describes the feeling of the students:

> *To us our eviction from the site bequeathed by William Morris for the Oxford Clinical School was more of a scandal than a controversy. In those buildings and gardens, we had felt nurtured and protected with a deep sense of contentment, belonging and in control. During that day we went through the stages of grief together, anger, denial and bargaining had all failed, so our only option was to move rapidly through depression to reluctant acceptance. Some key players posed for my camera, before we were moved into the Osler Portacabin in the car park. It was like a school playground two-classroom Portacabin – unbearably hot in summer, freezing cold in winter. We then moved into Osler's cubicle in the new John Radcliffe Hospital where we had just one room, entered off the canteen, but this provided no adequate facilities for medical students and it was an unpopular time during the move to the new John Radcliffe Hospital.*

As early as 1919 the Radcliffe Infirmary purchased the Manor House estate in Headington to provide sanatorium accommodation for tuberculosis sufferers. They had applied to the Radcliffe Trustees for the use of some of the Observatory land, but without success, and in the course of time the Manor House site was chosen for the new John Radcliffe (JR) Hospital. The Women's Centre (JR1) was opened in July 1972 and the acute hospital (JR2) in 1979.

Alastair Buchan was president of the Osler Club at the time and took on Doll very impressively. Dr John Ledingham and Dr Bent Juel Jensen were two doctors who acted as champions for the students. Alastair fought hard for use of the stable block of the Manor House on the new hospital site to be used by the students, but this was rejected and it was Alex Gatherer Director of Public Health and District Medical Officer in Oxford and Lady McCarthy Chairman of the Oxford Health Authority who offered the College the Dower House. This was originally occupied by Robin Anson Owen, the Deputy Administrator of the United Oxford Hospitals, later by senior physicians and finally by Dr John Badenoch, Consultant Physician and Director of Clinical Studies. It was a cost willingly paid for by the College but not one at that time they could really afford.

In 1975-76 the Dower House had become vacant and the Area Health Authority made it available to the students. It became William Osler House replacing Osler House on the former site in a similar vein to the Radcliffe Infirmary becoming the John Radcliffe Hospital.

When Green College was founded it was agreed with the Osler House Club that all members of Green College would automatically become members of the club. Some links remain, although on a more informal basis.

Boating successes

112

Appendix 1
Plants in the Green Templeton College Medicinal & Herb Garden

The plants are perennials, native to Europe unless otherwise stated. Their common names and times of flowering are given in parentheses.

1. Betonica officinalis (Wood betony; June-September)

Regarded since Greek times as a panacea for all ills. The Italians had a proverb 'Sell your coat and buy betony'. After listing 30 complaints for which it was suitable in *Botanologia: Tile British Physician* (1687), Robert Turner wrote 'More than all this has been proved of betony', and Apuleius wrote 'It is good whether for the man's soul or for his body'. Contains stachydrine and harpagide. Mostly traditionally used for headache, but also for jaundice, epilepsy, stroke, gout, dropsy, shortness of breath, fever, excessive sweating, and rabies, and as a vermifuge.

2. Ajuga reptans (Common bugle; May-July)

Ajuga may be a corruption of the Latin 'abigo' = 'I drive off' (referring to disease). According to Pliny, abiga was a kind of plant with the power to induce abortion. Ajuga was traditionally used to treat wounds, haemorrhage, coughs and haemoptysis (spitting of blood), dyspepsia, gall stones, quinsy, and alcoholic hangover. It contains many compounds, including ajugaside and harpagide.

3. Origanum vulgare (Marjoram; June-September)

The original ancient Greek word described an acrid herb; in manuscripts it was often written as originating from two words as if it came from a mountain brightness, joy, or pride. It contains the antifungal, antihelminthic compound carvacrol. Traditionally used for sore throat, colic, catarrh, and asthma. Also used as the culinary herb 'oregano'.

4. **Artemisia annua (Sweet wormwood; qinghao; annual ruderal Central Asia; July-Sept)**
A panacea of the traditional Chinese materia medica, first mentioned in a recipe manuscript of 168 BC. As a remedy against acute intermittent fevers it was first recommended by the Chinese herbalist and physician Ge Hong (284-363 AD), in a medical text, *Emergency Prescriptions Kept up one's Sleeve* (c. 340 AD). A cold extract of its leaves was shown to be antimalarial by the chemist Tu Youyou in 1971, who_was awarded the Nobel Prize in Medicine or Physiology in 2015. The active ingredient is the cyclic endoperoxide artemisinin or qinghaosu, semisynthetic derivatives of which (e.g. arteether, artemether, and artesunate) are now used in combination therapy in malaria.

5. **Anemone pulsatilla (Pasque flower; April-May)**
Used to colour Easter eggs, hence perhaps its common name, although it also blooms at around Easter time. Its active ingredient is ranunculin, a glycoside that is hydrolysed to protanemonin, a lactone with antibacterial activity. It has been traditionally used to treat cough in asthma, whooping cough, and bronchitis, as well as for headache, amenorrhoea, toothache, earache, measles, and nettle rash.

6. **Artemisia absinthium (Common wormwood; July-August)**
Named after Artemis, Greek goddess of the moon, to whom it was sacred. Absinthe is made from it. It was for a long time thought to be effective against poisons, such as hemlock and toadstools. Its chief ingredient is artemolin. Mainly traditionally used as a vermifuge and as a bitter, but also as a cerebral stimulant, and in indigestion, gout, and liver and gall bladder diseases.

7. Inula helenium (Elecampane; July-August)

A tautologous name, since 'inula' is a corruption of 'helenium', possibly from ⚬ Helen of Troy, who was picking it when Paris stole her, and whose tears made it spring from the ground. Contains inulin (used today as a test of one particular aspect of kidney function), and the antihelminthic drug alantolactone.

Traditionally used for coughs, gall bladder disorders, lung diseases (particularly tuberculosis), anorexia and dyspepsia, in various neuralgias, and as a rubefacient.

8. Tanacetum vulgare (Tansy; July-September)

From the Greek 'athanaton' = 'deathless', perhaps because it was used for preserving corpses, and was supposed to have made Ganymede immortal. Tansy cakes were used as prizes for Easter games, and were thought to purify the bodily humours after the rigours of Lent. Contains compounds called tanacetals. Traditionally used as a vermifuge, and for flatulence, amenorrhoea, epilepsy, sprains, and rheumatism.

9. Rumex acetosa (Sorrel; May-July)

'Acetosa' because it is bitter. The dried root has been used to stain barley water red to simulate wine. Its main constituents are the cathartic drug emodin, chrysophanic acid, and calcium oxalate, which gives it its bitter taste.

Traditionally used for scurvy, itch, ringworm, sinusitis, bruises, burns, jaundice, and kidney stones.

10. Aloe barbadensis Milleri (Aloe vera; July-August)

A tender succulent from Africa. 'Aloe' possibly from the Arab word 'alloeh' = 'a shining bitter substance'. Described by Dioscorides as being effective against skin complaints and for wound healing, for which it is still used. Widely taken traditionally as an anti-inflammatory, a stimulant of the immune system, and an antiseptic and antibiotic. It contains anthraquinones, mucopolysaccharides, and saponins.

11. Calamintha grandiflora (Calamint; June-August)

Literally 'beautiful mint' (Greek 'kalos') with large flowers. Believed to be good at driving away serpents. Traditionally used for flatulence, jaundice, fever, depression, convulsions and cramps, and as a vermifuge.

12. Linaria vulgaris (Toadflax; June-September)

Linaria from the Greek 'linon' = 'flax', so named by Linnaeus because he thought that the leaves resembled flax. The common name 'toadflax' comes from a fancied resemblance of the flower to a little toad. Its main constituent is peganine. Traditionally used for dropsy, bowel disturbance, cystitis, liver disease, scrofula and other wounds, and inflammation of the eyes.

13. Akhemilla vulgaris (Lady's mantle; June-August)

The term Alchemilla is connected with alchemy, and relates to its supposed magical powers. Many plants were associated with the Virgin Mary ('Our Lady') in the Middle Ages, because they were regarded as 'herbs of grace': i.e. herbs with great healing powers. Mostly used for treating wounds, but also for haemorrhage, vomiting, diarrhoea, and menorrhagia.

14. Nicotiana tabacum (Tobacco; annual from South America; July-October)

First introduced into Europe by the Portuguese Joan Nicot a French diplomat in 1560 and into England by Sir Walter Raleigh in 1586. Contains nicotine. Apart from its use in cigars, cigarettes, and snuff, it has traditionally been used to treat strangulated hernia, urinary retention, hysteria, worms, lead poisoning, and tetanus. Attacked in 1604 by King James I in' A counterblaste to tobacco', the ill-effects of smoking tobacco were first raised by the epidemiologists Sir Austin ('Tony') Bradford Hill and Sir Richard Doll in 1950 These ill-effects were subsequently proved by the work of the latter over many years.

15. Primula veris (Cowslip; April-May)

From the Latin 'primus' ='early', referring to their flowers. Widely used as a herb, especially in salads, and for making wine. Contains primulaverin and priverogerins. Supposedly good for the complexion. Also traditionally used as a sedative and antispasmodic, for headache, insomnia, anxiety or nervous excitement, muscular rheumatism, kidney complaints, and paralytic illnesses.

16. Leonurus cardiaca (Motherwort; July-September)

So-called from a fancied resemblance to a lion's tail. The term 'cardiaca' does not refer to the heart, but to its use as a cordial. However, it has traditionally been used for heart diseases (e.g. palpitation) and affections thought to be associated with the heart (e.g. fainting, neuralgia). It was thought to be effective against wicked spirits, and was also used as a diaphoretic, antispasmodic, expectorant, vermifuge, and tonic. Contains ajugoside, leonuride, and leocardin.

17. Echinacea purpurea (Coneflower; June-September)

A perennial plant from North America. From the Greek 'echinos' = 'a hedgehog', referring to the prickly scales of the flower head. Traditionally used to treat wounds and snake bites, it is now used as an effective remedy for colds, flu, and throat infections, to boost the immune system, and to treat depression. Parts used: roots and flowers as tinctures, extracts and powders. Contains echinacosides, polysaccharides, antiseptic and antifungal resins, and antibacterial and antiviral glucosides.

18. Tanacetum parthenium (Feverfew; June-August)

'Feverfew', from the Medieval Latin 'febrifugia', since it was used to treat fevers. Also traditionally used for hysteria, depression, nervousness, amenorrhoea, coughs and wheezing, and bites, and as a carminative and vermifuge. In modern times it has been shown to be an effective prophylactic in migraine. It contains many compounds, including tanaparthins and chrysanthemolide.

19. Persicaria bistorta (Bistort; June-August)

'Bistorta' = 'twice-twisted', from the S-shaped roots. Very astringent. Used as a styptic for internal and external bleeding. Also traditionally used in diarrhoea, mouth ulcers, diabetes, fever, jaundice, smallpox, plague, measles, and haemorrhoids. In the Lake District it is used to make a herb pudding called Easter Ledges or Easter-Mangiant.

20. Conium maculatum (Hemlock; biennial; June-September)
Perhaps derived from a Greek word meaning 'to whirl about', because of its effects on the brain when eaten. Notorious for having supposedly been used to execute Socrates, although the exact nature of the poison is not known. Its maculae were supposed to represent the mark of Cain. Its main principal is coniine, which is responsible for its toxic effects: weakness, drowsiness, nausea, vomiting, laboured breathing, paralysis, asphyxia, and death. It was traditionally used therapeutically as an antidote to strychnine, and in rabies, epilepsy, teething, Parkinson's disease, arteriosclerosis, prostatic complaints, coughs, and scrofula.

21. Genista tinctoria (Dyer's broom; June-September)
So-called because it yields a yellow dye, used to colour cloth or leather. Used herbally in skin diseases, dropsy, gout, and rheumatism. Contains cytisines, tinctorine, and anagyrine.

22. Prunella vulgaris (Self-heal; June-September)
Perhaps from the German 'braune' = 'quinsy' (which it was supposed to cure). Traditionally used as an astringent, for sore throats, an ulcerated mouth, internal bleeding, haemorrhoids, and headache.

23. Helleborus niger (Christmas rose; December-February)
Perhaps from a Greek work meaning 'to injure' and 'bora' = 'food', referring to its poisonous nature; in Latin 'niger' means 'black'. Its white flowers appear in the winter. It contains hellebrin, a cardiac glycoside, which has been used for treating dropsy. Also traditionally used as a vermifuge and for headaches, enteritis, amenorrhoea, and hysteria.

24. Daphne mezereum (Mezereon; February-March)
From the Persian word for Daphne, 'mazaryun'. Contains Mezerein and daphnetoxin. Daphne is toxic to humans, cats and dogs. It is traditionally applied to the skin to cause a blister, as a way of removing fluid from the body (e.g. in dropsy). Also for poisonous bites, skin diseases, bladder ailments, rheumatism, scrofula, syphilis, and neuralgia.

25. Colchicum autumnale (Autumn crocus; perennial corm, dormant in summer; September-October)
So called because it supposedly originated from Colchis (Medea's home). Contains colchicine, which is used today for the treatment of acute gout, although it has largely been superseded by safer, more effective remedies. Also traditionally used as an emetic and cathartic.

26. Humulus lupulus (Hop plant; July-September)
Latin 'lupus' = 'wolf', because, according to Pliny, when it grows among willows it strangles them like a wolf among sheep. 'Hoppan' is Anglo-Saxon for 'to climb'. Contains humulene, the antibiotic humulone, and the sedative lupulin. Used for brewing beer. Medicinally it was traditionally used to improve the digestion and appetite and for treating jaundice, heart disease, delirium tremens, bruises, rheumatic pains, nymphomania, neuralgia, and fits. Hop pillows are supposed to promote sleep and to cure earache and toothache.

27. Ricinus communis (Caster oil plant; tropical shrub grown in the UK as an annual; July-October)
Latin 'ricinus' = 'dog tick', from the shape and markings of the seeds. Contains ricinine, the purgative ricinoleic acid, and the highly poisonous lectin ricin, notorious as having been used to poison the Bulgarian diplomat Gyorgy Markov by umbrella tip. Caster oil is used as a laxative. It has also traditionally been used externally for ringworm and itch, and to increase the flow of breast milk. Other uses include the making of fly-papers, the cleaning of pictures, and several industrial chemical applications.

28. Aconitum napellus (Monkshood; May-July)

So-called because it was used as a poison for arrows (Greek 'akontion' = 'a dart'), or because i grew in rocky regions ('akone'). 'Napellus' is a turnip, in allusion to the shape of its roots. It contains the antipyretic drugs aconitine and aconine, napelline, and aconitic acid, which is also used as a plasticizer. Used by homeopaths for heart disease; also traditionally in lumbago, rheumatism, and fevers.

29. Angelica archangelica (Angelica; biennial; June-August)

A sweet flavouring and a medicine. Called 'angelica' supposedly because of its angelic properties, and archangelica because its leaves or wings were thought to be larger than those of an average angel. Traditionally used as tea in Scandinavian countries for fever, infections, and gastrointestinal disorders, and as a tonic. Its chemical compounds include coumarins and turpenes. Now used primarily as a flavouring. Essential oils from the roots are used in perfumery.

30. Thymus vulgaris (Garden thyme; June-August)

From the Greek 'thumon', from 'thuein' = 'to make a burnt offering'. It contains the antiseptic and preservative thymol. It was supposedly a favourite plant of the fairies (remember Oberon in *A Midsummer Night's Dream:* 'I know a bank whereon the wild thyme blows'), and was thought to endow the air with freshness, releasing its fragrance when burnt. However, it was associated with death, and the Romans used it to treat melancholy. It was also traditionally used for flatulence, coughs, sore throat, headache, drunkenness, and nightmares.

31. Corydalis cava (Hollow corydalis; tuberous plant, dormant in summer; March-May)

Greek 'korudallis' = 'crested lark', which its flower was supposed to resemble. Contains various alkaloids, including the dopamine receptor antagonist bulbocapnine. Traditionally used as an hallucinogen and in syphilis, scrofula, and menstrual disorders.

32. Digitalis purpurea (Purple foxglove; biennial; July-September)

So-called by the German herbalist Leonhardt Fuchs in 1542, because of the resemblance of its flowers to thimbles (Latin 'digitus' = 'a finger'). Contains cardiac glycosides (principally digitoxin), which slow the rate of the heart and make it beat more strongly. It was therefore traditionally used to treat heart disorders, such as heart failure. It was also traditionally used to treat fevers, tuberculosis, epilepsy, mania, and wounds of all sorts, including scrofula. Modem equivalents are compounds, cardiac glycosides, purified from other plants, typically digoxin from Digitalis lanata.

33. Hypericum perforatum (St John's wort; July-September)

From the Greek 'hyper' = 'above' and 'eikon' = 'a picture', referring to the tradition of hanging the plant above pictures to ward off evil spirits. 'Perforatum' because the leaves are dotted with tiny holes. Contains the pigment hypericin, flavonoids, and tannin. Traditionally used externally for minor burns and scalds. Still used today by mouth for mild depression, but may interact with other drugs, increasing their metabolism and thereby reducing their efficacy.

34. Catharanthus roseus (Madagascan periwinkle; tender perennial, South America; July-September)

From the Greek 'katharos' = 'pure' and 'anthos' = 'a flower'. The leaves contain anticancer compounds, the vinca alkaloids, three of which – vinblastine, vincristine, and vindesine – have been used in modern times, particularly in treating leukaemias and lymphomas. Other compounds it contains are vinleurosine and vinrosidine.

35. Vinca minor (Lesser periwinkle; March-May)

From the Latin 'vincere' = 'to bind', from its having long trailing stems that spread over other plants. It contains many vinca alkaloids, including the vasodilator vincamidine. Vinca minor has traditionally been used for haemorrhage, diarrhoea, cramp, and haemorrhoids.

36. Oenothera biennis (Evening primrose; biennial; June-September)
Perhaps from the Greek words meaning a wine-trap ('oinos thera'), because 'the roots ... are eatable, and were commonly taken after dinner to flavor wine' (William Baird; nineteenth century). Oil of evening primrose contains gamolenic acid, which has been marketed in modern times for use in eczema and mastalgia. It has also been used traditionally for functional gastrointestinal disorders, asthma, and whooping cough.

37. Atropa belladonna (Deadly nightshade; June-August)
Named after Atropos, the Greek Fate who cut the thread of life (in allusion to its poisonous nature), and supposedly from its use to enhance female beauty by dilating the pupils (Italian 'bella donna' = 'beautiful lady'), although that interpretation has been challenged. It contains the alkaloids hyoscyamine and atropine, which inhibit the parasympathetic nervous system. These and related compounds are used today as pupillary dilators, to speed the rate of the heart when very slow in some circumstances, and to treat motion sickness, and asthma. Homeopaths have used it to treat scarlet fever and cancer, and it has also traditionally been used to treat gout, rheumatism, circulatory collapse, and sore throat.

38. Malva moschata (Musk mallow; June-August)
Greek 'malakos' = 'soft'. Traditionally used for treating bruises, sprains, and aches, haemorrhage, dysentery, coughs, kidney stone, and stings.

39. Galega officinalis (Goat's rue; July-August)
So-called perhaps because its leaves emit an unpleasant odour when bruised. Contains galegine and peganine. Traditionally used in diabetes mellitus and to promote the secretion of breast milk. Metformin, which is chemically related to galegine, is used to treat diabetes.

40. Salvia officinalis (Common sage; July-August)
Latin 'salvere' = 'to be saved', alluding to its curative properties. Was supposedly effective against snake bites. Traditionally used for fevers,

delirium, typhoid, liver and kidney complaints, haemorrhage, sore throats, measles, amenorrhoea, and headache, and to clean and strengthen the gums. Culinary uses include its combination with onion as a stuffing for poultry, as a sauce or relish, and in a cheese made from rennet. Contains many compounds, including caffeic acid.

41. Dipsacus fullonum (Fuller's teazle; biennial; July-August)
Greek 'dipsios' = 'thirsty', because its leaves form deep cups which hold dew and rainwater. The heads of the flowers were used by cloth-workers (fullers) to tease cloth. It has traditionally been used as an eye-wash and to treat warts, wens, and jaundice.

42. Taxus baccata (European yew; long-lived tree; March-April)
Widely grown as a hedging plant and named 'baccata' or 'bearing red berries' for its characteristic fruits (poisonous). The related tree the Pacific yew was the source of taxol, which led to the development of the taxanes, such as paclitaxel and docetaxel, used as chemotherapeutic agent in the treatment of breast and other cancers.

43. Papaver rhoeas (Field poppy; annual; June-August)
Latin papaver. Many other plants were also called 'poppy' because children would blow up their flowers and pop them. Contains rhoeadine and papaverrubines. Traditionally used medicinally for catarrh and coughs. Also used for its oil, as a substitute for olive oil. Poppy seeds are used in baking, to decorate bread and in the cakes known as Hamantaschen ('Haman's ears') eaten on the Jewish festival of Purim.

44. Papaver somniferum (Opium poppy; annual; June-August)
Latin 'somniferum' = 'sleep-carrying'. Greek 'opos' = 'juice'. Contains the opium alkaloids, including codeine and morphine, used clinically as pain-killers and cough suppressants and to treat some forms of heart failure. Also contains the vasodilator papaverine. Heroin is a derivative of morphine.

45. Valeriana officinalis (Valerian; June-September)

Maybe from the Latin 'valere' = 'to be well'. Contains the alkaloids valerine and chatinine. Traditionally used as a sedative and tranquillizer, in epilepsy and cholera, and for strengthening the eyesight. Not to be confused with the more frequently occurring plant commonly referred to as 'valerian', which is properly Centranthus.

46. Foeniculum vulgare (Fennel; July-September)

Diminutive of Latin 'foenum' ='hay'. Traditionally used to counteract the griping action of purgatives, to stimulate lactation, as a carminative, and for coughs and inflammation of the eyes. It is also used in salads and honey. Contains umbelliferone and bergapten.

47. Phytolacca decandra (Poke root; N. America; June-July)

Greek 'phyton' = 'a plant', Latin 'lacca' = 'crimson lake'. Contains the alkaloid phytolaccine. Traditionally used for various skin diseases, headache, rheumatism, conjunctivitis, haemorrhoids, and cancers of the breast and uterus.

48. Chelidonium majus (Greater celandine; May-September)

Greek 'chelidon' = 'a swallow', because it flowers when the swallows arrive and fades when they migrate. Contains the alkaloids chelidamine, sparteine, and berberine. Used in jaundice, eczema, scrofula, scurvy, warts, ringworm, and corns, and to encourage sweating.

49. Hyssopus officinalis (Hyssop; June-October)

So called from the Hebrew 'ayzov', indicating its use to cleanse holy places. Traditionally used for rheumatism, bruises, lung diseases, flatulence, and hysteria. It is also used in perfumery. Contains pinanone.

50. Sallie alba (White willow; April-May)

Contains the analgesic salicin, which is related to aspirin (acetylsalicylic acid). Introduced for the treatment of agues (fevers) by the Reverend Edward Stone, from the English village of Chipping Norton, in 1763. Traditionally used for neuralgia, headache, rheumatism, cuts and burns, dyspepsia, diarrhoea, and dysentery, and as a vermifuge.

51. Ruta graveolens (Rue; June-September)
Greek 'ruomai' = 'to set free', alluding to its efficacy as a herb. Contains the coumarins rutaretin and isorutasin, which supposedly reduce the fragility of small blood vessels, and caprylic acid, which is used in perfumery. Medicinally it was traditionally used in coughs, croup, colic and flatulence, sciatica, headache, hysteria, and palpitation, and as a rubefacient.

52. Sambucus nigra purpurea (Purple elder; June-July)
Greek 'sambuke', a four-stringed instrument for which presumably the wood of this tree was used. The common name 'elder' is from the Anglo-Saxon 'aeld' = 'fire'. Traditionally used as a purgative and emetic, and in dropsies, epilepsy, asthma, bruises, and sprains. Its culinary uses include the making of wine, jam, vinegar, chutney, and ketchup. Contains campesterol, sitosterol, and stigmasterol.

53. Camellia sinensis (Tea plant; perennial shrub, Asia; April-May)
After the Latinized name ('Camellus') of the botanist George KameL of the late 17th century, when it first came to Europe. 'Tea' from the Chinese 'T'e', in Cantonese 'Tcha'. Contains the stimulant caffeine, and the diuretic theobromine. The green leaf contains catechins, which are oxidized by enzymes during fermentation to yield theaflavins and thearubigins. These impart the qualities known as 'brightness', 'briskness', 'body' and 'colour'. Catechins also give the astringency and bitterness characteristic of Chinese and Japanese green teas (unfermented or partially fermented (oolong) teas).

54. Borago officinalis (Borage; annual; June-September)
Said to be a corruption of the Latin 'cor ago' = 'I bring the heart', referring to its cordial properties, but more probably from 'burra', a shaggy garment, in allusion to its leaves. Used for fevers, lung diseases, inflammatory swellings, rheumatism, jaundice, itch, ringworm, and sore throat.

I

APPENDIX 2
THE GREEN TEMPLETON SUNDIAL

The Sundial works by using a spot of light cast by the nodus (the gilded sun with a hole in the middle), falling upon the slate dial-plate and tracking from left to right across it.

It is declining because the wall it is attached to does not face due south but 'declines' away from the compass point.

Noon-mark means it gives the point at which the sun at its zenith crosses the Greenwich meridian and the Oxford meridian (the vertical white line down the centre of the dial).

Mean-time means you can read clock-time from the dial by following the progress of the year along the figure-of-eight marking, known as an analemma or equation of time correction curve. This makes allowances for the effect of variations in the apparent motion of the sun at different times of the year.

The sundial also contains additional features:

Equinoctial and solstitial declination lines crossing horizontally, which show how the sun will track on the winter solstice (top line), spring and autumn equinoxes (middle lines), and summer solstice (bottom line).

Astrological symbols for the corresponding months.

Two white heraldic stars representing Venus and the Star of Texas[20] from the College Crest.

The title Meridies Media, meaning 'the middle of the day'.

---

20 The transit of Venus was linked to the building of the Radcliffe Observatory and Cecil Green made his money from Texas Instruments.

(a) Sunset over Hinksey Hill as seen from Professor Hornsby's dining parlour at the Observatory 20th December, 1784. The Equatorial Telescope House is seen to the left. (Ashmolean Museum Oxford)

(b) A later photograph of the Equatorial Telescope House

APPENDIX 3
EQUATORIAL HOUSES

There were several houses for telescopes that were built in the grounds of Observatory independent of the Observatory itself.

1. Around 1780 a small stone-built circular structure (photos (a) and (b)) was designed apropos the Temple of Romulus in the Roman forum. Its position is shown at the bottom left on the 1876 Ordnance Survey map (photo (c)) and its base can be seen in the aerial photograph of 1920 (photo (d)). It survived until the closure of the astronomical use of the Observatory in 1934 when it was demolished and its telescope was rehoused temporarily in the smaller 'Rotunda' by the Observatory.

2. The small 'Rotunda' next to the College was constructed in the 1840s.

3. In 1903 the 'Great Equatorial' came into service at the instigation of Arthur Rambaut. The term refers synonymously to the telescope (photo (e)) and the larger rotunda that was built to house it (photo (f)). A basic requirement of both rotundas was complete stability of the buildings and builders of the Great Equatorial went to great lengths to make the structure stable, as Arthur Rambaut reported in 1900 to the Radcliffe Trustees:

In the second week in December Messrs Parnell commenced the building of the Tower designed by

129

Mr Jackson. When the specified depth of 12ft was reached, we found ourselves in water-logged sandy gravel, altogether unsuitable as a foundation. I decided it would be best to penetrate the gravel, and embed a mass of concrete in the clay. It necessitated the use of a steam pump, working continuously day and night. At 17ft the character of the gravel improved very much. We were then 5ft below the water-level (about the level of the river at Medley Weir).

Both it and the small Rotunda are shown in photo (d). This Tower, without its domed roof, ended up lost amongst a group of miscellaneous hospital buildings until being demolished in the 1960s (photos (g) & (h)). This was an ignominious end to a building designed by the eminent architect TG Jackson.

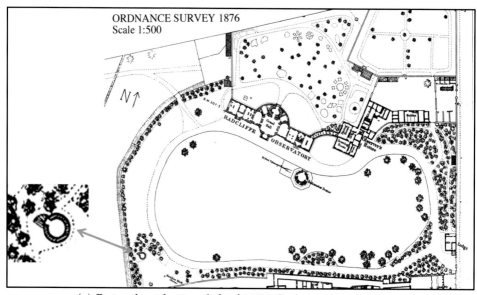

(c) Rotunda at bottom left of 1876 Ordnance Survey map

(d) 1920 Aerial view showing the base of the original Equatorial House

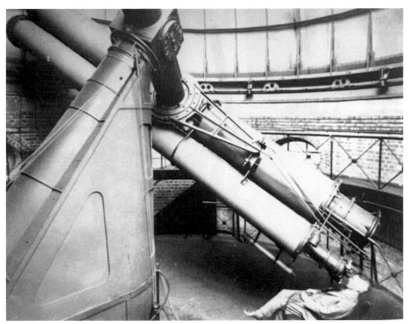

(e) The Double Equatorial Telescope of 1903 with Harold Knox-Shaw on the observing chair. Courtesy the Bodleian Library Oxford and the Radcliffe Trust

131

(f) 1922. The heliometer tower since 1907 which occupied the 10-inch Barclay refractor is centre, the much larger double equatorial tower is to the left.

(g) & (h) 1963 images of the second rotunda before and after demolition to make way for the Gibson Building

Other Books by David Cranston available from WORDS BY DESIGN

JOHN RADCLIFFE
and his Legacy
to Oxford

David Cranston
Illustrated by Valerie Petts

John Radcliffe and His Legacy to Oxford
David Cranston
978-1-909075-18-4 / 86pp / hb

"Dr Cranston has written a biography, as intriguing as it is scholarly, of one of Oxford's most remarkable benefactors. The incalculable benefits to science, medicine and architecture of Dr Radcliffe's largesse 300 years ago live on to this day and are an eloquent testimony to the vital contribution made by visionary philanthropy to the mission of a university: education, scholarship, research and the public good."
Sir Ivor Crewe, The Master,
University College

I am delighted as a physician to commend a book written by a surgeon about a physician.
Sir Roger Bannister CH

PENICILLIN
and the Legacy of
Norman Heatley

David Cranston & Eric Sidebottom
Illustrated by Valerie Petts

Penicillin and the Legacy of Norman Heatley
David Cranston and Eric Sidebottom
978-1-909075-46-7 / 100pp / hb

"At last, a biography of the crucial member of the Oxford research team that gave the world penicillin."
Professor Max Blythe,
Green Templeton College

"...the most human and humble person you could ever imagine, and his work on the development of penicillin will last for ever."
Paul N. Rimmer, Vicar of Marston, 1959-90

"It is remarkable that while his colleagues were receiving the world's acclaim for the development of penicillin, the crucial contribution of Norman Heatley was largely forgotten. What is equally remarkable is that, in subsequent years, he never expressed even a hint of disappointment or envy at his exclusion."
Sir James Gowans,
Fellow of the Royal Society

William Osler and His Legacy to Medicine
David Cranston
978-1-909075-48-1 / 132pp / hb

"William Osler was one of the founding fathers of the Johns Hopkins Hospital. David Cranston's biography will help to keep his name alive, and in these days of increasing technological advance remind all those involved in health care that humanity must remain central, and that, in Osler's own words 'the patient who has the disease is more important than the disease that has the patient'."

Prof Robert Montgomery, Formerly Director of the Comprehensive Transplant Center, The Johns Hopkins Hospital

Lord Nuffield and His Double Legacy
David Cranston and Peter Morris
978-1-909075-71-9 / 173pp / hb

"An incisive and comprehensive account of the extraordinary life of William Morris, Lord Nuffield. A rags to riches journey culminating in some of the most remarkable philanthropy of the twentieth century."

Professor Andy Carr

"David Cranston and Peter Morris tell the fascinating story of how this unpretentious, enigmatic man became one of the foremost industrial figures and philanthropists of the twentieth century. The work interleaves the story of Nuffield the man with a compelling account of the challenges, opportunities, up and downs of his times. Read and enjoy."

Professor Sir Peter Ratcliffe

Peter Morris and His Legacy to Transplantation

David Cranston

978-1-914002-39-7 / 162pp / hb

As a Surgeon-Scientist he was the real thing. Supremely competent in all he did, Peter Morris inspired us all. David Cranston tells the fascinating story of his remarkable life and times. Enjoy!

Professor Sir Peter Ratcliffe FRS

This is an enjoyable and enlightening read, peppered with fascinating nuggets which give a balanced insight into this determined man.

Martyn Coomer

What comes across are not just the achievements, but also the humanity of one of the most universally respected surgeons of his generation. It is a picture of Peter Morris that will be very familiar to all who knew him.

Professor Peter Friend